WHAT TO DO WHEN YOU ARE ABUSED BY YOUR HUSBAND

A BIBLICAL PERSPECTIVE

BY ROBERT NEEDHAM

& DEBI PRYDE

CONTENTS

One Cautions to Counselors and Pastors Involved in Abuse Cases 5

Two Understanding Abuse and Its Effects 21

Three Contributions to a Husband's Abusive Behavior 53

Four Questions Abused Wives Commonly Ask 87

Five Closing Thoughts for Victims 115

Appendix A Seeking Capable Biblical Counseling 131

Appendix B Information about Shelters for Battered Women 133

Appendix C Reporting Violent Abuse 137

Appendix D Church Involvement with a Serious Abuse Case 141

Appendix E The Serious Issue of Divorce 145

1

CAUTIONS TO COUNSELORS AND PASTORS INVOLVED IN ABUSE CASES

WE BELIEVE the brief statements and cautions in the opening section of this book to be vital, and believe they should be carefully considered before attempting to assist a spouse who apparently or obviously is being abused by her husband. While this first section is primarily directed toward those desiring to be of help to an abused wife, we believe it is extremely helpful for a wife to read it carefully as well. Many of the statements and biblical principles explained in this chapter give needed perspective and act as the foundation for further considerations.

BEWARE OF THE POTENTIAL DANGER

Beware of the real danger to counselors or pastors who get involved in abuse cases.

With dismal frequency, somewhere in the counseling process the abuser will "turn" on the counselor, sometimes viciously accusing him of either misleading or contaminating his wife's thinking to convince her that she is abused. Her husband will also likely deny that she is abused, which equals "fact" in his own mind. Because of these two very common realities in abusive marriages, it is wise to have at least two responsible people involved in the counseling to protect the counselor and the honor of the Lord Jesus Christ and the church.

By means of a parable, Christ said of discipleship in the kingdom of God, that we should sit down and count the cost (Luke 14:28). The cost of counseling abusers can be very high, including slander, harassment, and attempts at intimidation. In extreme cases, abusers have been known to physically attack those who have provided refuge for their wives and increase their abuse once they discover the wife has asked for help. If as a counselor you are not willing to pay this price (Matthew 5:10–13; 2 Timothy 3:12) and are not willing to persevere once counseling has started, it is kinder to abandon the wife to her danger than to raise her hopes for a solution, only to have them dashed if you "bail out" of the effort from fear of the abuser.

The authors of this publication earnestly urge anyone who intends to be involved to a significant degree, to be much in prayer for God's blessing on the counseling efforts, remembering that abusers almost always have developed formidable defensive, deceitful, and manipulative skills. The abuser may very well out-maneuver you if you are not resting on the Lord for the gift of discernment and care, and for the grace to help in time of need (Proverbs 3:5–7; 24:26; Hebrews 4:16). Truly this endeavor will highlight Christ's declaration, *"Without me, ye can do nothing"* (John 15:5c).

INITIAL ASSESSMENT

Be extremely cautious in your initial assessment of women caught in abusive situations.

A significant majority of severely abused wives have great difficulty understanding the reality that the mistreatment, cruelty, and manipulation that they have been subjected to, is actual abuse. In part this difficulty exists because there is usually a long history of the wife having explained away, in her own mind, the husband's demeaning, unkind, disrespectful, or even violent and cruel behavior. Some women who have been horribly abused speak of abusive incidents in "flat tones," almost as if this treatment is normal, and show little emotion. Others come in a state of sheer terror, obviously fearful and nervous about taking such a major step in seeking help. Many pastors and counselors have expressed deep regret that they did not take abused women more seriously at the outset of the counseling. These women often appear to minimize the problem resulting in the counselor misreading the seriousness of the situation or the severity of the danger she is in. Encourage the women who come to you for help to be completely honest with you, as you cannot effectively deal with the situation without accurate and complete information. Nevertheless, it will be extremely helpful if you will recognize and consider how difficult it is for most abused wives to understand, let alone articulate, what is happening to them.

ABUSE IS AN ANGER PROBLEM

Do not blame the abuser's anger and abuse on marriage problems, circumstances, or other people, including his wife!

The sins which have become habituated in the abuser are so well honed and so deeply ingrained that with rare exception, the single most difficult aspect of counseling an abuser is the task of instrumentally helping him face, admit, and biblically deal with his own sins. It is pointless to try to deal with sin problems in the marriage relationship until the abuser is willing and (by God's grace) able to deal biblically with *his own sins first* (Matthew 7:3–5). The abuser has convinced himself (and others) that his anger and related problems are a direct result of circumstances he did not bring about, or other people in his life (especially his wife) who have not dealt with him as he thinks he deserves. If you treat his anger problem as a marriage problem, or address problems in his marriage before the serious problem he has with anger, you will unwittingly contribute to this powerful self-deception. This approach will fail to help him see he would be angry in any circumstance, with *any* wife, and that anger is a sin that reveals problems in his own heart, rather than a sin caused by others, or problems (however real), outside himself (James 1:20; Colossians 3:8).

We respectfully urge you *not* to approach an abuse case intending to sort out blame and determine who caused what. That will be a guaranteed dead end. Especially be careful not to blame a wife for her husband's violence in any way! His "buttons are pushed" whenever he does not get what he wants or expects. It does not matter how successfully a wife fulfills an abusive husband's demands, he will continue to construct new demands and vent outrage when they are not carried out with perfection. She will have obvious sins and weaknesses, but these should be dealt with separately, when the husband is ready to work on his marriage, or at the very least, when she is in a safe environment and is emotionally ready to concentrate on her sins and weaknesses, as well as anger of her own that she may be experiencing.

Remember that there is *never* an excuse for violence or mistreatment no matter what problems exist in the marriage. The abuser must learn that God expects him to deal with problems in biblical and godly ways, and holds him responsible when he does not do so. Again, so long as the abuser continues to successfully shift blame and responsibility to his wife and to others, God will not grant the grace of repentance and the abuser *will not* be able to conquer his sin (Galatians 6:5–8). The counselor must acknowledge that the abuser's wife is not flawless, and she has obvious weaknesses, and of course sins. At the same time the counselor must *refuse* to imply these have in any way *caused* the husband's problem with abusive anger. His wife may also have retaliated to the abuse in angry, or even physical ways, out of self-defense or an overwhelming sense of helplessness. While this is not a godly response and needs to be addressed at the appropriate time, the abuser must not be allowed to claim his wife is "abusive too" as a method to justify his violence or "frustration." Remember that this is *not* first or primarily a marriage problem. Abusive anger is a devastating, life-dominating sin that affects every area of a man's life, including his relationship to God, to his children, to his wife, and to others including co-workers on the job. They are not the cause of his sin, but rather, they are those most affected by his sin, and the usual objects of his expressed anger.

CAUTIONS REGARDING SUBMISSION

Be extremely careful about the advice you give a woman regarding submission.

Pastors and other counselors face a great danger of contributing to a real catastrophe, as well as becoming guilty of serious biblical error, by telling an abused wife to go back to her husband and "suffer for Jesus' sake." Such counselors often use 1 Peter 3:1–6 as their justification for such counsel, failing to distinguish between a difficult, and/or unbelieving husband and one who is terrorizing a family. Assault and battery is criminal behavior, not simply sinful behavior. We have often observed women being counseled by Bible-believing pastors who tend to reinforce the erroneous notion that if the woman is submissive and loving enough, the abusive husband will change, without any other action or intervention, or that God will transform the marriage if the wife has the right motives, faith, and so on, often with reference to 1 Peter 3:1. Sadly, this is seldom the case unless serious, active intervention takes place. In many cases, the husband never repents and never experiences change, no matter how godly, loving, and submissive the wife is. (This issue will be addressed more fully later on.) Most godly women who return to their abusive marriages after an episode of violence, do so because they want to obey God and because they have a great hope returning will be the means of restoring the marriage and will make possible change in their husbands' lives. This is often tragically encouraged by sincere but untrained pastors, and ends up putting a burden of responsibility on the victim that is incredibly cruel and unsubstantiated by Scripture.

Hence, the message conveyed by many pastors is that God requires a woman to live in terror, and that to resist or not submit to the husband's abuse or criminal behavior is to disobey God and refuse to submit to God's work in her life. Women counseled this way come to believe the only way of gaining God's blessing and make possible God's intervention to change her husband is by suffering graciously at his hands. Thus, the abused woman becomes obedient to a misconception, a perversion of the Scripture, (in fact, a lie of the devil), perpetrated by the very ones God has ordained to protect her. She dutifully resigns herself to suffer passively, to her own detriment and the detriment of her husband and children.

Some Bible-believing pastors are so afraid of sanctioning any kind of separation (quoting 1 Corinthians 7:5), that they fear they are disobeying God if they encourage it for any reason whatsoever. They frequently state: "nowhere in the Bible does God sanction separation." Yet here is a situation where the duty to preserve life and to protect the helpless must take precedence over a wonderfully true principle that applies except when a wife, and sometimes even the children, are in real danger, spiritually, emotionally, and physically (Proverbs 2:24-25; Micah 6:8; Acts 20:35; Romans 15:1; 1 Thessalonians 5:14).

Pastors do well to remember that God never gives any human being absolute authority. Absolute, sovereign authority belongs to God and God alone (Matthew 28:18). We who believe the Bible have no problem believing our Lord gave an explicit command for us to go "into all the world and preach the Gospel to every creature." We understand this is not a suggestion, but a command given to every believer charging us to witness and speak boldly about our faith in Christ with the express purpose of seeing others come to a saving knowledge of Christ. We understand that passages such as Romans 13:1–4 and 1 Peter 2:13–14 command us to submit willingly to God ordained, governmental authority. Yet we also understand that this authority never supersedes the authority of God. We would, as believers who are submissive to a higher authority than civil government, continue to proclaim the Gospel message, even if our government forbade us to do so. We would cite, like Peter and Paul, the Scriptures which command us to obey God rather than man in such cases (Acts 5:29; 4:19–20).

Indeed, throughout the centuries, millions of Christians have suffered torment and laid down their lives, deliberately disobeying commands to stop preaching the Gospel.

In the same way, God gives pastors, elders, deacons, and church leaders a measure of authority. He tells believers to "obey them that have the rule over you, and submit yourselves: for they watch for your souls, as they that must give account, that they may do it with joy, and not with grief: for that is unprofitable for you" (Hebrews 13:17). Even so, the serious Bible student understands that no pastor or elder, deacon or church leader has been given *absolute* authority, which requires unquestioned submission of church members. God commands that we separate from a brother who is a "fornicator, or covetous, or an idolater, or a railer, or a drunkard, or an extortioner" (1 Corinthians 5:11).

Diotrephes was a pastor who was not content with the limited authority God gave to him, and demanded absolute submission, assuming authority over people and things that had not been given to him by God. He was malicious and cruel, and went so far as to throw people out of the church when they would not submit to his ungodly demands. John replied to Gaius, who undoubtedly suffered as a result of Diotrephes' cruelty, "Beloved, follow not that which is evil, but that which is good." No church leader ever has absolute authority that supersedes God's authority or the authority of the Word of God. If a pastor demand his congregation drink Kool-Aid spiked with cyanide, they ought to disobey his command and say, "It is written, 'Thou shalt not murder'!"

God gives husbands a measure of authority for the harmony of the home and care of the family. As God commands citizens to submit to judicial authority, and Christians to submit to church authority, He commands wives to submit to their husband's authority—in everything. Yet, like any other authority God commands that we submit to, it is *never* an authority that supersedes His own authority. A husband has no God-given right to command his wife to violate any command of God, nor does he possess authority that gives him the right to demand his wife submit passively to evil, or to destruction that he perpetrates. Indeed, it can be said that his authority over his wife is valid only to the extent that he exercises that authority in conformity to God's Word.

God does not require us to submit to a Hitler and kill innocent Jews. God does not require us to submit to a David Koresh or a Jim Jones and take our own lives. And God does not require women to submit to a wicked husband who unjustly and unscripturally jeopardizes his wife or his children.

OUR RESPONSIBILITY TO DEFEND AND PROTECT

Remember that God commands us to defend and protect those who are oppressed.

Our God is a God who not only loves justice—He is a God who *is* just. Justice and judgment are said to be the "habitation" of His throne. (Psalm 89:14) The Bible tells us, "To do justice and judgment is more acceptable to the LORD than sacrifice" (Proverbs 21:3). We are to love justice the same way our God loves justice and are commanded to stand on the side of those who are being afflicted unjustly. "Defend the poor and fatherless: do justice to the afflicted and needy. Deliver the poor and needy: rescue them out of the hand of the wicked (Psalm 82:3-4)." If we love God and love our neighbor, we will also love justice and exercise it faithfully. We will seek it, work for it, defend it and do everything in our power to uphold it.

If we, as shepherds over God's flock, ignore the cries of bleating sheep and allow the wolf to tear them in pieces, we can expect God's judgment upon our unfaithfulness. Consider the words of Isaiah and Jeremiah on this subject. "And judgment is turned away backward, and justice standeth afar off: for truth is fallen in the street, and equity cannot enter. Yea, truth faileth; and he that departeth from evil maketh himself a prey: and the LORD saw it, and it displeased him that there was no judgment (Isaiah 59:14-15). "O house of David, thus saith the LORD; Execute judgment in the morning, and deliver him that is spoiled out of the hand of the oppressor, lest my fury go out like fire, and burn that none can quench it, because of the evil of your doings (Jeremiah 21:12)."

CONFUSION AND FEAR

Be aware that abuse almost always generates severe confusion, distress, fear, and guilt in the mind of the victim.

Many abused wives have later described it as a dense fog that only lifted as truth began to penetrate their mind and heart. It is an experience shared by those who have been prisoners of war or have been kept in isolation for an extended amount of time. Without guidance or rescue, an abused wife and children will learn to cope in several destructive ways, and will develop explanations and defenses that are consistent with a lack of understanding. The human heart is inclined to deceive itself and choose destructive or sinful ways of dealing with life's problems—particularly when life's problems are beyond the scope of one's understanding or ability to stop. Abuse sets in motion a variety of thoughts and fears, conclusions and resolutions that, left unchallenged or uncorrected, have the power to mold and shape the victim's mind and attitude in many hurtful ways years after the abuse has ceased. Thus, the biggest problem and potential for destruction lies within the responses of the victim's own heart, not within the power of the abuser. A compassionate counselor who effectively counters the lies of the abuser with the healing balm of God's truth throws a lifeline to the victim who is drowning in confusion brought on by the relentless tirades of an abusive spouse.

The greatest damage that is done to the victim of any kind of abuse is not to her body, as difficult as that is, but to her mind and soul. What she has come to believe, how she has been deceived, how blame has been shifted onto her, and how God's truth has been twisted and maliciously misapplied, all inflict inner wounds that are far more long-lasting than wounds inflicted upon her body. Perhaps a greater wound is the anguish brought upon a victim when she is not believed or protected by others that she goes to for help and refuge. Yet even more troubling than these is the torment of hearing the typical denials and protests of innocence made by the perpetrator if she attempts to expose him. It is no surprise that the one longing desire shared almost universally by victims is the desire to hear their abuser admit what was done and simply acknowledge his sin. It is extremely rare for an abuser to accept responsibility for his anger and cruelties without blaming, minimizing or excusing his sin.

JUDICIAL AUTHORITY

Lastly, we would caution all who come to the aid of an abused wife not to reject the help of judicial authority when a crime has been committed.

There is a significant difference between an offence that is to be dealt with privately and a crime which is to be handled by judicial authority. When there is clear evidence that a crime has been committed against a wife or children, it is a mistake to minimize it, cover it up or deal with it as something other than a crime. Some Christians imagine this is somehow merciful to the offender and easier for the victim. Both are grave errors. The Bible never condones a cover-up for any reason, particularly when a crime has been committed (Proverbs 28:13—He that covereth his sins shall not prosper: but whoso confesseth and forsaketh them shall have mercy. See also Leviticus 26:40-42). Rather, God has instituted our judicial system to deal with offenders who commit evil crimes against the innocent in society. The Scriptures declare that authority is ordained by God for our good (Romans 13:1-5). To ignore God's methods and attempt to deal with assault and battery crimes secretly is not only an egregious error, but is unkind to both the offender and the offended. It further traumatizes victims, fails to bring criminals to justice, and ultimately fails to bring criminals to repentance as well as forfeiting the spiritual credibility of the visible church.

If the crime of abuse is reported and the abuser is found guilty, he will likely be required to attend an anger management class and receive a set number of hours of counseling. It is often possible for a pastor to petition the judge and have all counseling and instruction handled through the church counseling ministry.

It is so common for church leaders to assume that no good can come from involving the civil authorities in a case of severe abuse that ministers, counselors and pastors sometimes not only violate civil statues concerning the reporting of a crime but also rob the church of the legitimate leverage for constraining an abusive husband in submitting to counseling he would otherwise reject out of hand. We cannot overemphasize the responsibility of church leaders to be aware of applicable statutes regarding spousal and child abuse and to seek to work with transparent cooperation with responsible local authorities. (police, child protective services, etc.) when it is appropriate to do so.

It is not uncommon for abuse to be covered up to such an extent that there is no documented evidence of violence that would serve as protection for a wife and children in the event the abuser seeks a divorce and custody of children at some later date. Remember that in a court of law, he who has the most documentation wins. Inferences, second-hand reports or accusations without evidence are not considered. A journal that provides an accurate timeline can be an invaluable asset. Keep all pictures of injuries or damage to property, text messages, voice mail messages, counseling records, emergency room records, physician reports, police reports, and so on, in a designated file in a secure place. These often make the difference between supervised visitation and equally shared custody of the children.

> *Ezekiel 34:2–10 says, "Thus saith the Lord GOD unto the shepherds; Woe be to the shepherds of Israel that do feed themselves! should not the shepherds feed the flocks? Ye eat the fat, and ye clothe you with the wool, ye kill them that are fed: but ye feed not the flock.*

> *The diseased have ye not strengthened, neither have ye healed that which was sick, neither have ye bound up that which was broken, neither have ye brought again that which was driven away, neither have ye sought that which was lost; but with force and with cruelty have ye ruled them.*

> *And they were scattered, because there is no shepherd: and they became meat to all the beasts of the field, when they were scattered. My sheep wandered through all the mountains, and upon every high hill: yea, my flock was scattered upon all the face of the earth, and none did search or seek after them.*

Therefore, ye shepherds, hear the word of the LORD; As I live, saith the Lord GOD, surely because my flock became a prey, and my flock became meat to every beast of the field, because there was no shepherd, neither did my shepherds search for my flock, but the shepherds fed themselves, and fed not my flock; Therefore, O ye shepherds, hear the word of the LORD; Thus saith the Lord GOD; Behold, I am against the shepherds; and I will require my flock at their hand."

2

Understanding Abuse
and Its Effects

Ellen was in tears for the umpteenth time when she called her good friend Patty to tell her that Jim once again had left the house in a towering rage, calling her unprintable names and threatening to leave her and the children. Once again Ellen wasn't quite sure what had triggered Jim's tirade. She had merely asked if he would be coming home for lunch. As in so many other incidents, Ellen's simple question or efforts to communicate with Jim were countered with personal attacks, shouting, name-calling, or threats. When Patty again urged Ellen to go to her pastor for help with the problem, she was reluctant, fearing Jim would carry out his threat to leave her if she did so. She also feared that her pastor would not believe her, because Jim had been a deacon in the church for years and everyone in the congregation who knew him thought that he was a model Christian. "No," concluded Ellen, "I can't risk embarrassing my husband. Besides, Jim has never actually hit me."

The first time William hit her in the face, Susan was almost paralyzed with fear that he would hit her again, and more severely. However, despite his anger and violence, William looked quite shocked at the realization of what he had done. He had bruised Susan's arms, slapped her, and pushed her on numerous occasions, but this was the first time he had hit her in the face. William quickly spun around and stomped out of the house, slamming the door behind him. Susan sat weeping hysterically for almost half an hour before she began to rationalize his behavior. Wiping tears, she began to think, "Well, he *has* had problems at work, and he really *is* a nice guy at heart. I know he didn't mean it because he really does love me. I'm sure it won't happen again. I just need to try harder to be a better wife."

Mary, a naturally trusting and unsophisticated person who delights in pleasing others, began to wonder why Henry would not seek out or initiate affection or physical contact with her for long periods, but then would unexpectedly demand her body. She puzzled about his growing sarcasm, biting remarks, and long periods of the "silent treatment" without admitting to any problem. Mary pleaded with Henry for an explanation, but the more she pleaded, the more he ignored her. Mary began to feel guilty over some real or imagined offense she couldn't identify, and often wondered if she had an emotional or spiritual problem. She even began to re-evaluate the unhappy memories of a disastrous honeymoon, wondering if she had deeply offended her husband then. Mary longed to go to a sympathetic pastor and pour out her heart, but she couldn't. Henry is also her pastor! "Perhaps if I just trust the Lord more," Mary sighed, "things will get better."

UNDERSTANDING ABUSE

If we think of wife abuse to consist only of severe beating, we will have tragically missed the point. In each of these three cases, the abuse springs from exactly the same underlying problems, even though it varies in intensity and in the manner it is expressed. All of these wives are subject to real and serious abuse by their husbands, and if uncorrected, it is almost certain to get worse. Consequently, it is very important to define abuse wisely, and respond to it appropriately.

Webster's 1828 Dictionary provides an excellent definition of the word, *abuse*. Abuse is an improper treatment towards another when one abuses his natural powers, privileges, or advantages. An abuser is one who "mistreats another in speech, or behavior; one that deceives; uses rudeness of language, ill treatment, or violence towards another person." While dictionary definitions certainly help us determine the accurate meaning of the words *wife abuse,* it is imperative for Christians to recognize that the Word of God must always be our final reference. Therefore, let us define *abuse* in light of God's Word as well.

The Bible recognizes that anger, rage, harshness, name-calling, cynical and sarcastic speech, fighting, and physical attacks of every sort constitute a serious mistreatment (abuse) of others. However, when we talk about abuse in the sense of a husband abusing his wife, we are referring to abusive behavior, as described in Scripture, that has become habitual, excessive, and destructive to the extent it has the potential of doing great harm to a wife and/or her children, either emotionally, physically, or both. It is a mistreatment used to control or overpower a wife in such a way that she is not able to function as an autonomous person.

THE WAY OF THE SPIRIT

- *Love which "worketh no ill to his neighbor" is the outcome of obeying the Spirit for the benefit of God's glory and the good of others. (Ephesians 4:29-32)*

- *God's love and grace move us to sacrificially give what is needful and good for the benefit of another. (Philippians 2:3-4)*

- *Christ sacrifices Himself to protect and provide for our need. (Philippians 2:5-8)*

THE WAY OF THE FLESH

- *All abuse is the outcome of satisfying the flesh [sinful human nature] at the expense of others.*

- *The abuser selfishly sacrifices another to satisfy his own wicked lusts and love of self.*

FROM A BIBLICAL PERSPECTIVE, ABUSIVE BEHAVIOR:

- *Comes from an undisciplined soul (Proverbs 16:32; 25:28).*

- *Reveals a proud and unteachable heart (Proverbs 16:18; 1 Samuel 25:2-38).*

- *Includes the failure to recognize one's responsibility for disciplined, careful, and righteous speech under all circumstances (Proverbs 10:11,14; 12:18–19, 22; 14:25; 15:1, 4, 28; 16:13, 21, 27–28; 17:4,20,28; 18:13, 21; 19:1, 28; 21:23).*

- *Comes from a heart that is rebellious toward God and His commandments (Psalm 2:1–3).*

- *Is characteristic of the "foolish" [rebellious] person described throughout Proverbs.*

- *Is characteristic of the works of the flesh and absence of the fruit of the Spirit (Galatians 5:19–24).*

- *Is characteristic of those who live "according to the course of this world, according to the prince of the power of the air, the spirit that now worketh in the children of disobedience: among whom also we all had our conversation [behavior] in times past in the lusts of our flesh, fulfilling the desires of the flesh and of the mind; and were by nature the children of wrath . . ." (Ephesians 2:2–4).*

- *Often ultimately reveals the heart of an unregenerate person who is engaged in persecuting one who is a child of God— just as Isaac, the child of promise, was persecuted by Ishmael, the child born after the flesh (Galatians 4:22–29).*

CHARACTERISTICS COMMON TO ABUSERS

Abusive men (and women) come from every walk of life, every income bracket, and every race and culture. With rare exceptions, friends, family, and business associates never guess or suspect wife abuse by the abuser's behavior in their presence. On the outside, the abuser rarely looks or acts like someone we would normally associate with such cruel behavior. He can be the one we call the life of the party or the one who seems shy, soft-spoken, and unassuming. He can be the cocky and outspoken new Christian, or just as easily, the beloved deacon or elder devoted to long hours of serving others.

The details vary from case to case and the individual cruelties of wife abusers differ even as personalities and circumstances differ. Nevertheless, several very common, yet tragic, sinful behaviors with almost no exceptions underlie genuine wife abuse. Some of the manifestations of sins that typically feed abuse include hidden selfishness, insecurity, extreme self-centeredness, fearfulness, explosive anger, immaturity, excessive jealousy and defensiveness, to mention but a few. The way this sin expresses itself may vary, but the ultimately causative sin of pride and the underlying sins are still very much the same from case to case. We will address some of these specific sins and look at how they develop and become so powerful. For the moment, it is important to first determine if a wife is truly in an abusive situation, or if she is overly sensitive and being overly critical of her husband.

It is not uncommon for some women to exaggerate their husband's offenses and believe they are abused when in fact they are not. On the other hand, many wives who are severely and genuinely abused feel guilty for even considering the possibility that their husbands are abusive. It is very helpful for women in these rather difficult situations to compare their husband's behavior with a checklist of known behaviors common to abusive husbands. In this way, they can discern more accurately the severity and true nature of their husband's behavior towards them.

Before you read the suggested checklist that follows, please understand that not every husband who is an abuser commits every one of these sins. Similarly, not every husband who commits one of these sins is an abuser. But if more than a few apply in any case, we may properly conclude that the husband is abusive to the degree that immediate help is needed if the marriage is to survive and grow. If you are willing to consider the possibility that your husband is dangerously abusive, prayerfully ask yourself the following questions, marking the boxes that apply to him.

☐ *Does his behavior, without warning, swing between loving, kind, and charming one day to cruel, explosive, and hateful the next?*

☐ *Is he extremely critical of your efforts, particularly if you are happy or enthusiastic?*

28

- *Does he blame you for his failures?*

- *Does he react angrily if you cry or express emotional distress or dismay when he is accusing you?*

- *Is he extremely jealous of your friends and family?*

- *Does he wrongly accuse you of improper interest in other men?*

- *Does he expect you to account for every minute you are out of his sight, particularly when you leave the home?*

- *Does he consistently disregard or discredit your views, feelings, interests, and preferences?*

- *Does he shove you around, bully you, or handle you roughly during a disagreement?*

- *Does he slap or hit you when he is angry?*

- *Does he grab your arm or neck roughly or painfully?*

- *Does he verbally attack or shout very loudly at you when he is angry?*

- *Does he become remorseful after an abusive incident, and try to be kind after being very angry, then begin to get cold and increasingly irritable as the tension builds, until he explodes all over again?*

- *Is he unreasonable or unapproachable during discussions?*

- *Does he threaten you with loss of the children, or other "punishments" if you confide in someone else about your problems?*

☐ *Does he appear to "punish" you with long periods of cold silence?*

☐ *Does he ever state, or imply, that he needs to "teach you a lesson"?*

☐ *Is he very sarcastic and defensive with you if you try to discuss any of his problems with him?*

☐ *Does he harshly belittle your accomplishments or your physical appearance?*

☐ *Does he call you demeaning names such as "stupid," "fool," and so on?*

☐ *Does he react inappropriately or angrily, or claim to be offended or "hurt" by your errors or faults?*

☐ *Does he isolate you from friends or family?*

☐ *Does he insist on completely controlling the finances so you have little or no discretionary funds?*

☐ *Does he resent the time you spend talking to friends or family members?*

☐ *Does he become very angry over trifling infractions of his arbitrary rules?*

☐ *Does he require you to get his approval of every purchase, no matter how small?*

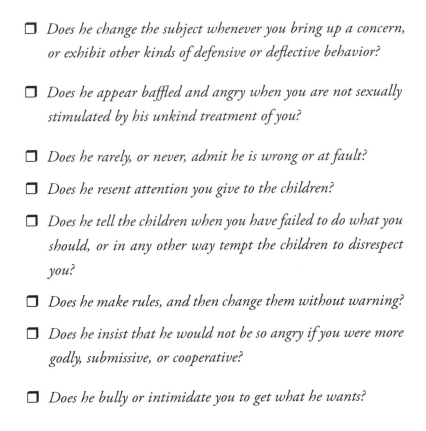

- ☐ *Does he change the subject whenever you bring up a concern, or exhibit other kinds of defensive or deflective behavior?*

- ☐ *Does he appear baffled and angry when you are not sexually stimulated by his unkind treatment of you?*

- ☐ *Does he rarely, or never, admit he is wrong or at fault?*

- ☐ *Does he resent attention you give to the children?*

- ☐ *Does he tell the children when you have failed to do what you should, or in any other way tempt the children to disrespect you?*

- ☐ *Does he make rules, and then change them without warning?*

- ☐ *Does he insist that he would not be so angry if you were more godly, submissive, or cooperative?*

- ☐ *Does he bully or intimidate you to get what he wants?*

EXTREME DEFENSIVENESS

One of the most common characteristics of an abusive person is a passionate defensiveness that takes on many forms. An abuser will vehemently deny he is abusive and will react to any attempt to confront him honestly with such forceful or skillfully manipulative denial that he successfully prevents disclosure or interference with his behavior, sometimes for a lifetime. This kind of person does not admit wrong. In fact, he seems to have a violent emotional reaction to mere suggestions he might be wrong, let alone sinning. Even when he admits mistreatment of his wife or expresses sorrow for his violence, it will be done grudgingly, or to get her "off his back," or with a deep-rooted belief that he mistreated his wife because she deserved it or provoked it. He convinces himself (and others) that his wife's deficiencies and sins are the basis for his mistreatment of her, thus relieving himself of any guilt or responsibility for the abuse. An abuser who is exposed will often go to incredible lengths to rally people around him, and will masterfully convince those who take his "cause" that he is being unjustly accused. People who do not understand the powerful deception and manipulation that accompanies abuse will often be seduced into the abuser's desperate attempts to justify and defend himself, further damaging whatever efforts are being made to bring him to a place of genuine repentance and restoration. Deflecting attention away from his unreasonable behavior becomes a well-honed skill. Defensiveness can include, but is not limited to:

- *Emphatic denial*

- *Blame shifting*

- *Clever twisting of a wife's words so that in any confrontation she ends up as the party at fault*

- *Sudden shifting to a "poor me" routine which can include crying (e.g., "I just can't do anything right as a husband. You're so critical of me.")*

- *Changing the subject when his wife attempts to confront him with a sin.*

- *Refusing to talk when his wife tries to address a concern.*

- *Sulking*

- *Flying into a rage (adult temper tantrum)*

- *Threatening wife with some serious harm if she continues to press the issue*

- *Demanding exhaustive evidential verification with specific incidences of his sin before he will entertain the possibility of any sinful speech or action*

- *False accusations toward his wife, accusing her of abusive actions toward him, or judging him. In men with Bible knowledge, it is common for the abuser to confuse the matter of judging, which is forbidden (Matthew 7:2), with evaluating behavior of another, which is commanded (Matthew 7:15–20)*

- *Cleverly twisting Scripture to confuse or undermine a wife's confidence in her ability to think biblically*

- *Misapplying Scripture to stonewall her expressed concerns about his behavior*

- *Stressing her duty to be submissive without any qualifying or modifying truth. [No human being may demand absolute submission of another. Only God has that prerogative. We have a duty to refuse to obey any unbiblical command (Acts 4:19–20; 5:29). God never commands a husband to make his wife obey him. This obedience is to be a voluntary act of the wife out of love and obedience to God.]*

FAMILY INFLUENCE

Another revealing occurrence in the lives of abusers is the frequency with which abusers share the experience of having been raised in homes where their mothers, or other women, were treated with disrespect or violence. The fact that an abusive man's father was abusive, in no way excuses his mistreatment of his own wife, and it in no way predetermines that he will be an abuser himself. Not all men raised by abusive fathers become abusers, but a significant majority of abusers were raised by abusive fathers or mothers. Abusive behavior is learned as a young boy watches the way his father treats his mother, and makes a series of choices as to whether he approves or disapproves of this behavior. It is learned as he listens to his father rationalizing and comes to believe that the father's excuses and justifications for the abuse are legitimate.

As a son craves the love and approval of his father and determines to act in a way that will win his father's acceptance or mark him as a man in his father's eyes, he is tempted to imitate his dad. Abusive behavior is learned as a young boy hears his abusive father shift blame for the abuse onto others, and onto his mother. It is learned as he sees his father place a burden of guilt upon others without a biblical understanding of God's gracious provisions and mercy for sin.

Anger is a habit easily learned, which is why God warns, *"Make no friendship with an angry man, and with a furious man thou shalt not go; lest thou learn his ways and get a snare to thy soul"* (Proverbs 22:24–25).

THE CYCLICAL PATTERN OF ABUSE

Abusive husbands commonly follow a cycle that is incredibly predictable. Nevertheless, until the classic cycle is pointed out to both the abused wife and the abusing husband, neither usually recognizes the pattern nor realizes how common the cycle is to an abusive situation. Usually it takes a wife several "cycles" before she realizes what is taking place and begins to understand it is not a problem that is getting better, nor a problem that will go away without serious intervention. Rather, it will happen again, and again, and again if it is not thoroughly, biblically, and carefully dealt with.

Following is a description long recognized as the typical, cyclical pattern of wife abuse:

1. *Build-up Phase—Gradual build-up of tension, irritability, verbal cruelty, cold silence, and unhappy countenance.*

2. *Blow up Phase–Usually the abuser generates a major issue from some small incident, (e.g., wife forgot to pick up laundry, leaves a light on, didn't iron a shirt perfectly, etc.) verbally assaults his wife, and then reacts to her protests (or silence) with increased anger, culminating in physical violence and/or an extremely hurtful verbal attack.*

3. *Remorse Phase–The abuser "feels" some remorse (what the Scriptures call "worldly sorrow") after mistreating his wife and tries to "make up" for his cruelty by being exceptionally kind or generous. He will not be able to sustain this*

superficial kindness demonstrating that his remorse is not biblical repentance.

4.   *Build-up Phase—Gradually the abuser's fleshly remorse and stated commitment to be kind fades and tensions build until the abuse is repeated*

An abusing husband, with rare exceptions, will "feel" some level of remorse after he has mistreated his wife … maybe the next day, maybe immediately, maybe some days later. He may strongly believe he is repentant and will never "lose it" again. This kind of abuser makes promises and may express "horror" over what he has done until he convinces his wife it will never happen again. Other abusers aren't so anxious to acknowledge they have done anything cruel or unjustified. One way or another, they may ask the wife for forgiveness or lamely hint they are "sorry," but admissions of guilt are very vague. Most often, the abusing husband will never actually admit he was wrong, and if he does, it will be accompanied with reasons he believes his behavior is justified. If he's the type who never accepts personal responsibility or admits fault, he may act as if absolutely nothing of consequence has happened and put on the "Mr. Nice Guy" front. The wife will initially be uncertain, but as the "niceness" continues, she will talk herself into believing the problem is solved.

The abused wife eventually recognizes the "Dr. Jekyll-and-Mr. Hyde" personality of her husband, but convinces herself he is himself when he is calm, and being *unlike* his real self when he is "stressed" or "frustrated." What she fails to realize is that his behavior when angry and provoked reveals the true condition of his heart (the real self), and not the other way around. After a period of time (from either a few days, or a month, or more) some little incident will occur, and the husband will begin to display the corruption that dominates the hidden heart, and the abuse will be repeated, almost always with increased thoughtlessness, harshness, or violence. He can only maintain the show of niceness for so long. His willpower and resolve are no match for the power of sin that lies hidden in his heart. Inevitably, his true heart attitude will surface again and again with surprising and often escalating fury (Matthew 12:33–37; 15:10–20).

Many abused wives have realized, in retrospect, that in each of these cycles of abuse, there was a gradual buildup of tension before the next explosion occurred. They couldn't always put their finger on it, but they often sensed when a violent outburst was coming and felt powerless to do anything about it. Some express relief when he "gets it over with." When their husbands finally did explode, they note that his rage nearly always involved some real but minor failure on her part. Sometimes the offense was very inconsequential and truly trivial, though it had a crumb of legitimacy. This allowed the abusing husband to justify his abuse in his own mind, deflecting blame to his wife even though his response to his wife's behavior was monumentally disproportionate to her real or imagined offense.

With each cycle of abuse, the mistreated wife will be devastated. Many, though not all, abused wives begin to wonder if they are "going crazy" and begin to question their own sanity or their perception of what has taken place. This will be even more agonizing if the husband denies any wrong on his part, "forgets" the incident, or cleverly reinterprets what has happened. His habit of "rewriting history" blurs reality and makes the abused wife question what she heard or saw. The emotionally wrenching abuse cycle keeps a woman in a state of constant turmoil, distrust, and confusion, weakening any ability to respond biblically or to think clearly.

IMPACT OF ABUSE ON A WIFE

Self Doubt—Confusion

The degree to which the husband has managed to isolate his wife, (not only from others, but from truth itself), tends to increase her internal struggles as she experiences abuse and as she seeks to make sense out of what has happened or is happening daily. She may have great difficulty discerning the reality of her husband's manipulation and abuse because she has no one else with whom she can test her perceptions. Proverbs 11:14 speaks of this: "Where no counsel is, the people fall: but in the multitude of counselors there is safety." Generally, her emotional state becomes such that reading Scripture offers little comfort because she immediately convinces herself that she is not interpreting a passage correctly if it offers her hope and direction. If the husband is a professing Christian, he will probably reinforce her uncertainty by suggesting she is incompetent in discerning Scripture or is in rebellion against Scripture and therefore rejected by God.

Gradually, the abused wife will lose her ability to accept her own perceptions or come to any conclusions on her own, and will believe she is incompetent in every area of her life. This instability and confusion make it difficult for an abused wife to act independently of her husband or to maintain distance from him long enough to clearly discern what is actually taking place. She tends to be the kind of woman who wants to be led and well taken care of. If she is a committed Christian, she may also sincerely want to be submissive to her husband. Because she wants to believe the best about her husband, she is easily manipulated and led into emotional paralysis and inaction. She tends to easily conform to her husband's thoughts and interpretations over God's Word and the mind of Christ.

False Guilt—Learned Helplessness

A wife who has been abused for some time usually will doubt whether she can do anything right. She will immediately feel guilty the moment she is criticized, even if the accusation is wickedly unjust, or takes place in the presence of frightened and bewildered children. Eventually she comes to believe she cannot survive apart from the abuser or to stop the destructive effects the abuse has on her and the family as a whole. This process of learned helplessness paralyzes a woman emotionally (particularly in her capacity to make decisions) and is one of the reasons so many abused wives experience great difficulty making enough of an emotional break with the husband to get the kind of help they both need.

The abusing spouse becomes adept at blaming and accusing his wife to relieve himself of guilt or blame. The more an angry husband fails to deal with his own sin and guilt, humbly and biblically, the more he seizes upon every opportunity he can to point out failure on the part of his wife. This steady barrage of criticism and faultfinding begins to erode the confidence and discernment of a weakened and spiritually frail wife. It ultimately leads her into taking responsibility for her sins as well as the sins and failures of her husband, as her husband defines them, rather than how God defines them. This unquestioned acceptance of guilt that did not originate with God's Spirit, distorts her understanding of God's promises and character. A woman in this situation allows her husband to take the place of God in her life, and allows him to exert authority over her that God never granted to him. The more she accepts and resigns herself to this kind of destructive attack, the more bold and confident will be her husband's demeaning accusations. He desperately wants to believe he is not at fault and is only angry because someone or something other than himself is causing the anger. This false belief leads him further away from truth and makes it impossible for him to acknowledge that it is his own demands and expectations that fuel his anger. In other words, well-intentioned caving in to an abusive husband's treatment of her actually subsidizes and reinforces his false beliefs and determination that she accepts blame for his sinful behavior. She ends up unwittingly perpetuating the very tragedy that she grieves over and that is destroying the potential for a loving, God-blessed marriage relationship.

Fear

An abused wife is typically fearful, not only of her husband, but also of saying anything negative about her husband to a pastor or counselor. She often fears that she may be committing a terrible sin of disloyalty in seeking help. As a result of the husband's threatening and highly manipulative behavior, the wife is conditioned to believe that she is betraying her husband, and maybe even God, by daring to suggest that her husband is anything other than wonderful...daring to suggest he is sinning against her... even daring to think that maybe he needs help.

A wife who has repeatedly experienced the terror of being assaulted, threatened, and cruelly berated by a raging, out-of-control husband, correctly recognizes the very real danger this situation puts her in. If she stays, she risks being assaulted and beaten. If she attempts to leave, she risks even greater violence, which may escalate to murder, whether accidental or deliberate. Most deaths that are attributed to wife abuse occur immediately following an attempt on the part of the wife to leave the husband. Many women do not have sufficient resources, whether financially, socially, or emotionally, to take the necessary steps to protect themselves and their children if the husband reacts with violence and rage. Understandably, this possibility leads to fears that are both real and exaggerated.

Living in an atmosphere of prolonged fear and constant tension in a prepared, on-guard state, drains a wife of her enthusiasm, energy, and hope. It often robs a woman of her health and emotional strength and produces effects not unlike those seen in people who live in a war zone. Because the abuser's behavior is alternately abusive and non-abusive, a wife is never sure what response to expect from her husband, and thus, can never gain a sense of security or peace in the relationship.

Wrong Desires and Beliefs vs. Biblical Truth

A person's behavior and response to mistreatment is consistent with what she believes and desires in her heart. For example, if a woman believes she deserves the mistreatment of her husband, she will respond by resigning herself to it. If she believes God is judging her for a past sin(s), she will experience the despair of rejection. If she believes she can prevent her husband's anger and abuse, she will knock herself out trying to do everything just right to prevent an outburst. If she believes she cannot survive without her husband, she will not attempt to separate for any reason. What we believe and what we desire in our hearts has the powerful ability to drive what we do, what we say, and what we think. In the end, it will determine profoundly the outcome of our behavior, and will result in joy or sorrow. Only the truth of God has the power to set us free from wrong desires or wrong beliefs (John 8:31–32,36). A wife believing she cannot survive without her husband, in fact, is the sin of idolatry.

To experience God's power and victory in an abusive situation, a woman must bring her desires and beliefs into harmony with the mind of Christ, not the mind of her husband. Each destructive misbelief needs to be replaced with the healing truth of God that truly sets a believer free. God's truth is a hope-producing Biblical alternative to believing or desiring that which leads to despair. Desiring a husband's approval over God's approval, or relying on human reasoning rather than biblical truth, leads a woman to be sinfully dependent and weak. In contrast, a woman who learns to give God first place in her heart learns how to love her husband in ways that are pleasing to God, and learns how to confidently discern both good and evil (Hebrews 5:14). A discerning counselor is able to show an abused woman how to recognize the many sinful and destructive desires of the flesh that prevent her from responding to abuse in a confident, loving, and godly manner. A good counselor will also be able to show the abused wife how to be transformed by the renewing of her mind through believing and appropriating the truth of God's Word, and learning to depend on the ever present grace, comfort, and power of the Holy Spirit (Psalm 107:19–20; Psalm 146:3; Romans 8:35–37; Romans 12:2, 21; 1 Corinthians 10:13–14; Hebrews 4:15–16). As a mistreated woman learns to draw close to the Lord Jesus Christ and find her strength and guidance in Him, she will find Him to be altogether sufficient to guide her through whatever difficult trials lie ahead.

Some of the most common debilitating desires that keep mistreated women in emotional bondage are:

- *"I want peace, no matter what it costs."*

- *"I want someone to take care of me, even if he causes me pain."*

- *"I want a person I can depend on, even though God has told me to put my trust wholly in Him."*

- *"I want to enjoy the emotional feelings of being loved and cherished by my husband, even if he mistreats me and even if the emotional feelings represent trust in a false system of love."*

- *"I want the security of familiarity in my life, even if it destroys me."*

- *"I want a solution on my own terms, even though my solutions have always failed."*

Some of the most common misbeliefs that distort a mistreated woman's judgment are:

"I deserve this mistreatment."

Biblical Response: In the sense of the theology of redemption from sin, in the finished work of Jesus Christ, and of the fallen nature of man, I truly *deserve* all the miseries of this life, of death itself and all of the torments of hell forever. However, no husband ever has the right or privilege to abuse his wife as an administration of judicial correction on behalf of God. Judicial punishment belongs to God alone in the spiritual sense (1 Peter 3:7; Ephesians 5:25–33; Luke 6:22–23, 26).

"God is judging me/rejecting me."

Biblical Response: Deciding that a particular difficulty, trial or persecution is a direct evidence of the Father's judgment or rejection on one's self or another, is one of the most evil of all theological corruptions. It is also one of the first addressed in detail in the Bible, specifically in the book of Job as the heresy expressed by Job's three friends and by Christ's response to the apostles when they asked about disasters which had befallen others (Job 1–42, especially 1:1–13 and chapters 38–42; Psalm 103:10–17; Luke 13:1–5; Matthew 5:10–12 and 7:1-2; 1 Peter 4:12–13; 2 Timothy 3:12; Romans 8:1, 33–39).

"If I could do better, I would not be mistreated."

Biblical Response: This idea, while seemingly righteous and seemingly humble, is in fact demonstrably unbiblical since true righteousness, as indicated above, actually invites persecution and mistreatment. Evil men will behave in evil ways whether Christians "do better" or not. It can even be a subtle form of works righteousness on the part of a wife to actually believe that her "goodness" in and of itself can be a God blessed instrument in reforming her husband. This kind of thinking can be indicative of a wife who sees herself as a "rescuer" which is a sinful misapplication of 1 Peter 3:1(2 Timothy 3:1–5; John 5:5; Proverbs 14:12; 28:6; 2 Corinthians 3: 5–6; 1 John 3:13; Matthew 5:10-12; 10:34–39).

"Perhaps he is right and my failures cause his anger."

Biblical Response: A husband's unrighteous anger is caused only by his sin nature and only on rare occasions by the direct involvement of Satan, and that, only with the unsaved. A wife can behave so sinfully that she tempts her husband to be angry with her, but his anger against her is still his sin; and he cannot justly blame her for his sin (Ecclesiastes 7:9; 1 Thessalonians 5:15; Titus 1:15–16; Romans 6:1–2; 14:12; Proverbs 22:24–25; 19:19; James 1:19–20; 2 Corinthians 5:10).

"It is easier to agree with or endure my abuser's accusations and verbal attacks than to disagree with him or defend myself in any way."
Biblical Response: Of course it is "easier" in the short haul to agree with an abusive person's accusations, verbal and or physical attacks. However, passive acceptance, with very few exceptions, tends to stimulate an increase of rage on the part of the abuser. Bullies like to bully those whom they can easily intimidate, and every abusive husband is, in fact, a bully. Many times a bully will behave more brutally or with cruelty toward a victim who submits, interpreting that submission as cowering that "proves" the abuse is "deserved." The Scriptures tell us, *"If it be possible, as much as lieth in you, live peaceably with all men"* (Romans 12:18), but sometimes, that is simply not possible (Jude 3; 2 Samuel 13:1–13; Romans 13:12; Proverbs 18:21; 2 Thessalonians 3:13).

"If I submit to this mistreatment with a loving and good attitude, God will help me and intervene."
Biblical Response: Submitting to unjustified, impermissible evil is *never* blessed or righteous, not the least because it means the abuser is reinforced in his habituated wickedness, as well as being passively encouraged to lose out on God's intended blessings promised to husbands who cherish their wives as Christ cherishes His church (1 Peter 3:7; Luke 17:3–4; Ephesians 4:14–16,25;

Romans 13:14; James 5:16,19–20; Proverbs 28:23; Proverbs 27:5–6).

"If I do not willingly submit to my abuser's mistreatment, I am disobeying God."
Biblical Response: Being persecuted for righteousness' sake (i.e., our confession of Christ and our walk with Him) does not obligate us to passively receive or to submit to evil without resistance, but rather, the Scripture obligates us to overcome evil, actively. (Ephesians 4:11 and 5:14). To be unwilling to expose a husband's abusive behavior is actually a profound lack of Christ-like love toward him and a selfish putting of one's own short-term safety ahead of his-long term spiritual good (Romans 12:21; Proverbs 27:5–6; 25:26; Isaiah 5:20; Acts 4:19; 4:29; Revelation 2:20).

"A meek and quiet spirit means I'm to say nothing and accept blame."
Biblical Response: If this is true, then Moses was regularly in sin for all the times he strongly confronted sin, both in Pharaoh and later on, in the Israelites. Yet Scripture testifies that he was one of the meekest men that ever lived. Taking blame for another's sin is not only unrighteous, but is actually idolizing him and denying him the God-commanded feedback he needs to repent. Saying nothing and accepting blame can also be an expression of understandable fear, and an unwillingness to trust God to bless obedience in difficult circumstances. Meekness is not passivity. Meekness is, rather, the essence of humility. A quiet spirit does not describe one who does not speak up, but one who has an inner

peace with God and security in God's love (Romans 15:13–14; 2 Corinthians 4:1–5; 10:1–6; James 1:2–3).

"Submitting to authority means I should not question or resist one who is in authority over me."

Biblical Response: Whenever anyone in authority commands of us that which is clearly contrary to the Word of God, it is sinful to submit, and in fact, it is our solemn duty to resist that evil. Our resistance is not to be with fleshly weapons but with spiritual (2 Corinthians 10:3–5), carefully avoiding sin in attitude and manner, but resistance nonetheless. No greater an example than that of Peter, James, and John has been given to the church for the rest of time in their refusal to obey the sinful commandment of the Sanhedrin to refrain from preaching the Gospel (Acts 4:19; 5:21).

A husband's authority over his wife is *never* absolute, but legitimate only to the extent that it conforms to the Word of God. This in fact is true of all human authority and of all humans in a position of authority, although it is incumbent upon each one to be very careful in not rejecting authority lightly or in a sinful manner (Romans 13:1-7). Demonstrating biblically that a worldly commandment is sinful falls upon the recipient of the command (Romans 12:2; Jeremiah 17:5).

"I could not endure the shame of exposing this person's sin."

Biblical Response: If we are ashamed of exposing the sin of another (see Luke 17:3–4), it is likely because we are afraid that our own sins may be brought to light as a result of the confrontation (i.e., being counterattacked), or we are ashamed of our failure to have wisely chosen our spouse in the first place. To be ashamed of exposing sin is to be willing to tolerate evil and actually is a sin of pride because to do so requires humbling oneself. Exposing sin is difficult because most people don't like being confronted. Confrontation takes effort and faith. If we really believe someone else's sin is his and not ours, the "shame claim" is a shallow excuse that is actually theologically irrelevant (Romans 3:9–20, 23; Romans 6:23; Matthew 7:11).

"No one would believe me if I described this mistreatment."
Biblical Response: Sadly, this is often the case, even in good, Bible-teaching churches. Well-meaning church officers, fellow believers, and family members may well be unwilling to believe the testimony of an abused wife, especially if her husband is well respected in the church and even more so if he is an elder, deacon, or pastor. Further, an abused wife may well be accused of slander, as may the counselor if he or she seeks to help her (Colossians 3:1–25). Regardless of this difficult possibility, a godly wife is still obligated to resist sin, even in the midst of difficulty (1 Peter 3:1; 1 Peter 2:18-25).

"I could not survive without my abuser."
Biblical Response: This is both idolatry and the sin of unbelief. This error reveals evidence of an unwillingness to trust the Heavenly Father and is the same kind of fearful unbelief that characterized the Israelites whom God destroyed in the wilderness. (Psalm

78:41) The minute people think they cannot survive without another person as their insurance for one or more kinds of security, they commit a terrible kind of idolatry. In so doing, they deny the sufficiency of God as well as impugn His character concerning His declared faithfulness and His promises to those who love and trust Him with their souls (2 Corinthians 4:7–9;16–18; Hebrews 13:5–6; 1 John 5:21; 4:18–19).

"I must have a man to care for me."
Biblical Response: This simply and plainly contradicts the Scripture and in particular, the power and sufficiency of Christ's shepherding love for those whom He has saved (2 Thessalonians 3:3; Acts 17:24–26; James 1:16–18; Luke 11:23).

"I am incapable of surviving alone."
Biblical Response: The comments for errors #12 and #13 apply equally here. Such statements are the voice of cowardly unbelief, man-centered thinking, and the abject sinful fearfulness that characterizes those who are not willing to exercise faith in God (Deuteronomy 31:6–8; Jude 24–25; Revelation 21:8; Luke 9:23–24).

"If I could express myself better or explain things better, the person who is mistreating me would see how much he is hurting me and stop."
Biblical Response: This is truly fleshly, secular thinking, as if God's supernatural blessing on my feeble and flawed efforts in *anything* depends on my own developed, verbal confrontational

skills and not upon God's righteous character, loving grace, mercy, and strengthening that is given to every believer in Christ Jesus. Spiritually dead people cannot see anything spiritual no matter how much or how well those spiritual truths are explained Note that Scripture makes it very clear that very angry people have a flat learning curve (Proverbs 19:19) (Ephesians 2:1–10; 1 Corinthians 2:12–14; John 3:1–5).

"If I upset my abuser, he might kill himself and I could not live with the knowledge that I caused his death."

Biblical Response: The person who believes that speaking the truth in love (Ephesians 4:15) causes a suicidal person to commit suicide (self murder), displays an enormous error in discernment. It is preposterous to believe that one's speaking has more causal weight in determining another's choices than in the self-murderer's own corrupted thinking. Suicidal people typically commit suicide when they are angered that others will not cater to their wants, agendas, and so on. They believe that this final act of rebellion against God's sovereignty will manipulate their survivors into wishing they had provided that catering. Others who commit self-murder do so when they convince themselves their situation is hopeless, and want to prove to others their situation is hopeless.

Again, the action stems from one's own sinful thinking, unbelief, and unwillingness to submit himself to God, not from hearing the truth. A wife who believes she can cause another's choice of suicide cowers in fear and withholds from her husband the very thing he needs most—truth (John 8:31–32; Galatians 6:4–5;

Romans 14:12; 1 Corinthians 3:8; Matthew 13:10–16).

"If I can show this person how much I love him, I believe he will change."

Biblical Response: This is charming sentimentality and disguised arrogance. People change because the loving grace and mercy of God in Christ Jesus is brought to bear on their lives through the instrumentality of the supernatural power and working of the Holy Spirit. All other apparent causes of change are secondary instrumentalities employed by our Sovereign God to accomplish His divine purposes by sanctifying us despite ourselves (John 15:5; Romans 16:25; Hebrews 13:20–21; 1 Peter 5:10; 2 Peter 1:3; 2 Timothy 3:1–16; 1 Timothy 2:16–17; Philippians 4:13).

3

CONTRIBUTIONS TO A HUSBAND'S ABUSIVE BEHAVIOR

GUILT

One of the common characteristics of abusive husbands is their strong inclination to manage their guilt using unbiblical methods. All people "manage" guilt by one or more man-made means or methods, unless they have come to know and receive the Biblical truths of the Gospel, particularly the truth about God's forgiveness of sin through the finished, redemptive work of Jesus Christ alone. Rather than repent, confess, or make right wrongs committed against God or others, people often attempt to drown out guilt with over-activity, drugs, alcohol, or immoral indulgences. They may deny, justify, or compensate for their guilty conscience with impressive good works, or they may blame others. Most often, however, people will find some way to punish themselves (even if indirectly and unwittingly), and attempt to "work off guilt" by some form of behavior that is self-afflicting. This form of guilt management may include transferring the guilt to another person by treating the loved one in a very cruel way that is not altogether dissimilar from the Old Testament practice of laying hands on the sin-bearing sacrificial animal, and then killing it.

The guilt that results from specific sins is removed only when genuine repentance toward God and others has been exercised, *even after salvation* (Acts 26:19-20). The substitutionary sacrifices of the Old Testament were only a picture of the one true sacrifice God promised would come—Jesus' substitutionary death on the cross to bear the punishment that sinners justly deserve. Even in Old Testament times, God made it clear that nothing other than faith alone in God's great sacrifice has the power to free man from the effects of sin and guilt (Genesis 15:6). Nothing is able to adequately relieve a guilty conscience except God-given faith and repentance toward God, as God defines repentance. It cannot be relieved by the good works we do to make ourselves look good, by giving the sacrifices of our time or money, or by enduring hardships serving Christ. Though guilt may produce a subtle desire in our hearts to blame others and inflict pain upon them, it can never be quenched by doing so. These methods of guilt management give, at best, momentary relief. In the end, they increase guilt rather than diminish it, and prove to be unsatisfying to the troubled heart of an abuser.

Blaming others for our own sin is one of oldest forms of trying to control guilt (Genesis 3:12–13). It is resorted to, in part, because the blamer does not want to face his own sin, yet often senses he must somehow deal with it. If he can convince himself others are responsible for his anger and his problems, he can avoid having to face up to his own tormenting sins and guilty conscience. He will convincingly distort reality so that others, not himself, are at fault in the theater of his own mind. Because our human minds are sinful by nature, even after we are saved, and because our thinking can become very convoluted and self-deceived (Jeremiah 17:9), it is possible for the human mind to live with unforgiveness and guilt if someone else is being punished for one's own guilt. However, this path invariably leads to sin that begets more sin, and results in increasing cruelty and unreasonable behavior toward the sacrificial lamb "recipient." Men who abuse their wives as a result of their own failure to deal with guilt biblically are capable of abandoning all restraint and becoming deadly in their treatment of others. They are also destined to suffer untold anguish and torment in the hidden corners of their hearts for their lack of mercy (Matthew 18:34–35). It is not uncommon for abusers to be severely depressed or anxious.

Managing guilt apart from humble repentance for sin and the seeking of God's forgiveness is always unbelieving and therefore, evil. It is always rebellious against the Word of God, and it always does injustice to the sufficiency of Christ's forgiveness and the acceptance and restoration to God's fellowship that comes as a result. Consequently, people who manage guilt using unbiblical methods have an inadequate understanding of the magnitude of God's love and forgiveness, or their own faulty perception of it. They often express worldly sorrow over their sins rather than true repentance. Worldly sorrow results in a fleshly, self-centered "apology" unaccompanied with any true humility, change of heart, or change in direction. True repentance, on the other hand, always results in humility, a change of heart, a willingness to admit wrong without being defensive, to express specific repentance for specific sin, a strong desire to seek forgiveness, an eagerness to make wrongs right, godly sorrow for offending Christ and grieving the Holy Spirit, and other observable fruits of repentance (Psalm 51:17, 2 Corinthians 7:10–11).

The God-given grace of repentance is commonly misused by an abuser who wants to hide an unrepentant spirit or escape the discomfort of genuine repentance. When his sins are blatantly undeniable and he is pressed to repent by his wife or others, he may immediately interrupt discussion by declaring, "I repent, so do you forgive me?" The godly wife, trying to be Christ-like and remembering Matthew 6:14–15 or Luke 17:3–4, forgives him, whereupon he refuses to discuss the problem further and proclaims that any subsequent discussion means she has not forgiven him. This deceptive and manipulative behavior is in contrast to that of a genuinely repentant person who is willing to see the offense through the victim's eyes and eager to come to terms with the full extent and underlying implications of his guilt and sin. He wants a clear conscience and knows that this will be given by God only when he is in complete agreement with God as to the impact and wickedness of sin. The truly repentant person will spare himself no emotional or spiritual sorrow or agony in facing his own sin with thorough honesty. (Psalm 32:1-5, Psalm 51:1-17)

PRIDE

The second major contributor to abusive behavior is the age-old sin of pride. Because pride is so badly misunderstood in our post-modern, anti-biblical age in which we live, we need to begin by defining it Biblically and carefully.

From a Biblical perspective, pride includes . . .

- *The attitude of arrogance, the absence of true humility and the haughtiness of spirit, all of which are always sinful (Proverbs 6:16–17a; 8:13; 11:2; 15:25, 33; 16:5, 18–19; 18:12; 29:23).*

- *The refusal to humbly admit specific sins, ask forgiveness, or make restitution (2 Corinthians 7:9–10; 12:21).*

- *Thinking more highly of one's self than one ought to think (Romans 11:20; 12:16; 1 Timothy 6:17; 1 Corinthians 10:12).*

- *Believing one's self to be more important than others, or than God says we are (1 Corinthians 13:4–5; Philippians 2:3–8).*

- *Believing that one can rebel against God and His Word without consequence (1 Samuel 15:1–23).*

- *Taking credit for gifts, abilities, inherited characteristics, or accomplishments that are clearly gifts of God (John 15:5c;*

> *2 Corinthians 10:17–18; James 1:17, Galatians 5:25–26;*
> *6:3, 14; Proverbs 27:2).*

- *Boastful speech (Psalm 75:4–5).*

- *Refusal to live in humble dependence upon God for every-*
  thing (I Timothy 6:3-5; Proverbs 21:4).

Prideful people rob God of His rightful prerogatives of recognition as the giver of *every* good and perfect gift (James 1:17), and of their duty to worship Him in spirit and in truth (John 4:23–24). Instead, the proud in heart lust for the recognition, approval, or adoration of others. They are not primarily concerned with God's glory, but rather, seek to establish their own glory. Prideful people sometimes have a consuming desire to be thought well of, even if it is not a reputation justly deserved. They wish to be praised for what they have not accomplished, and they commonly make the effort to garner recognition that is not merited. A common expression of this kind of pride is a jealousy of others who do, in fact, accomplish worthwhile things. A prideful and fearful person who is selfish and self-centered cannot stand to have others praised or thought of more highly than himself, for he will regard that as robbing him of the center of attention which he craves. Prideful people have great difficulty living with another person who is more competent or intelligent than they are, even if only in one or two areas of life.

By definition, a lust (i.e., a fleshly desire for control or self-exaltation) is an appetite that controls us instead of our controlling the appetite. All desires, when met in an unbiblical way, prove to be insatiable and unsatisfying appetites. Consequently, the person who is seeking to get personal recognition and affirmation in an ungodly way will become increasingly insensitive to the rights and feelings of others, and will grow to demand that others recognize him, appreciate him, cater to him, concede to him, and submit to him. As this sin progresses and consumes a person's life, increasingly he will become more bold and arrogant in his demands and manipulative means of acquiring recognition. A prideful person will eventually come to resent anyone who does not cater to his immature and essentially lustful ego. Yet for all his effort and demands to maintain the preeminence he so greatly desires, the prideful person finds that joy and peace elude him. He doesn't realize he fights against God, for indeed the Scriptures warn, *"God resisteth [is opposed to] the proud, but giveth grace [desire and ability to do God's will] unto the humble"* (James 4:6). It is worth noting that the Puritans wisely regarded pride as the root sin from which all other sins arise.

When one does not respond agreeably to an abusive person's lust for adoration and control, he will criticize, slander, and ultimately reject them. In fact, if he is sufficiently hardened in heart, he is likely to ruthlessly attempt to destroy anyone who threatens to expose him or prevent him from having his own way. Like the playground bully, he threatens and intimidates those weaker than himself to get what he wants. And when threats do not work, he commonly resorts to pouting (even crying), manipulating, controlling, or deceiving. In the case of an abusive husband, he will demean and abuse his wife because he knows she knows him as no one else does, and he fears and hates her ability to identify his failures, weaknesses, inconsistencies and sins. He will try to dislodge her perception of his sinful behavior by treating her like a princess one minute ("See, I'm really a lovable guy and I think you are wonderful") to worthless the next ("You are the despicable cause of my behavior and your perceptions can't be trusted"). His wife's "behind the scenes" knowledge makes him painfully aware that she is not so easily convinced. Hence, she is often the target for blame and the most demeaning attacks on her credibility and confidence. With rare exception, once an abusive husband realizes a friend or counselor sees through his veneer and recognizes what he is like "behind the scenes," the latter will receive similar treatment from the husband even though it may be tempered somewhat in its outward expression. An abusive husband blindly refuses to believe that the efforts to confront him truthfully about his behavior are out of deep concern and love for him by all who attempt to help him.

An abusive husband typically deceives others with his outward charm, flattery, and manipulation to ensure they will admire and praise him. He works tirelessly to build and project a facade of respectability, sincerity and spirituality while maintaining self-will, selfish desires and prideful ambitions. Pride causes an abuser to maintain such profound self-love and self-interest that he is willing to sacrifice all that is precious in his relationship with his wife and children on the altar of his own agenda, his personal wants, his presumed needs, and getting his own way in any matter of importance to him. This prideful desire for self-gratification can lead to a misuse of money and family resources, a misuse of sex, a misuse of time, and a misuse of one's body. It can also lead to a terrible misuse of a man's own wife and children.

The abuser's pride fuels his judgmental behavior toward his wife and others he interacts with. He has little or no tolerance for the faults of others, critically magnifying them while at the same time minimizing his own faults and insisting on forbearance and patience for himself. He can be deeply wounded and even enraged if someone even suggests the existence of a modest fault, deficiency or sin in his life. His judgmental manner of thinking causes him to contradict his wife when her views differ from his, and assert his own view no matter how much evidence exists opposing it. Even when the abused wife provides a legitimate and understandable reason for some action she has done, he will contradict her and arrogantly assert that he knows better than she does why she has done what she has done. Often he will go so far as to declare he knows what she is thinking (when she has not told him), and assigns pejorative motives to her thinking and actions that are nothing more than his own speculations and distorted presumptions projected on her. Any attempt by the wife to give a true explanation of her motives and thoughts, or any attempt to correct his perspective results in intense objections, accusations or violence. No effort to reason with him produces a change of heart. If anything, it only intensifies his denial and abuse.

Incredibly, pride is so blinding that the prideful person almost never recognizes his own obvious problem with pride. The Scriptures verify this conclusion in its passages describing a prideful person. It is interesting to note that in almost every instance which an example of pride is given, the prideful party does not recognize his pride (e.g., Luke 18:9–14). It is accurate to say that, to the degree pride takes root in an angry man's heart and insidiously dominates his thoughts, speech and behavior, he will become self-deceived and blinded to his sin. He will come to a place where he can defend and hang on to his sin so tenaciously that he is not able to recognize criminal behavior in himself, such as assault and battery, rape, attempted murder, or murder. It is not unusual for an abuser to maintain his innocence and explain away his violence as something other than a crime, even with a battered wife lying at his feet, bruised and unconscious. Police officers have responded to domestic violence calls only to find the batterer weeping over his murdered wife, crying out, "I didn't mean it! I'm not a bad person! I love my wife!" Such is the frightening ability of pride to blind the mind and distort one's perception of guilt.

In one highly publicized abuse case in the Los Angeles area, it became clear that respectability was extremely important to the accused abuser. So arrogant was he, and so good was his facade of innocence that the public engaged in heated debates over his culpability in numerous well-documented incidents of violence toward his wife. He was so incredibly good at making himself look sincere and innocent that reasonable, intelligent people believed he was a "good guy" incapable of murder, *even though the evidence pointing to his guilt and murder was overwhelming and obvious.* To the humble man, truth is more important than respectability. The proud man finds it easy to sacrifice truth on the altar of self-love, and relentlessly pursue his own desires and perceptions, however selfish or however false.

ANGER

A third major contributor to wife abuse is anger. All human beings struggle with expressed or unexpressed anger to some degree, for all of us have a heart prone to wanting our own way and a heart prone to deceiving ourselves into believing we deserve what we want (Isaiah 53:6). It is this basic *internal* heart problem that produces sinful expressions of anger. External situations may cause the anger of the heart to surface, but they do not cause the anger in the heart. Sinful anger, the Bible tells us, comes from within the corrupted nature of the man, not from situations arising outside the man (Mark 7:23). We cannot blame the injustices or the failures of others, or the difficulties and tragedies of life, for our anger and mistreatment of others. God holds us responsible for the way we react to these things, and does not excuse sinful retaliation or vengeance on the basis that someone has wronged us or has failed to meet our expectations. Even when we are mistreated, we are to overcome evil with deliberate, active, good responses. Any attempt to overcome evil with evil ends in destruction and does not elicit the blessing of God (Romans 12:14–21).

Accepting and responding to the natural disappointments, difficulties, injustices, failures, and irritations of life in a godly, trusting manner does not come naturally to human flesh. God's own children often have a hard time believing God can use even the most painful experiences for their own good and His righteous purposes. They have an even harder time completely entrusting themselves to His wise and loving shepherding care. The unbeliever, on the other hand, cannot even fathom living by this principle. He does not live according to faith in God's Word or in the person of Jesus Christ, but he lives and responds according to his own foolish, darkened way of thinking. Responding as Christ responded to life's trials is a discipline of grace that God gives to believers as they learn what it means to live in harmony with, and dependence on, the Holy Spirit Who indwells every true child of God (Galatians 5:16–17).

One mark of a true believer is a deep desire to be like Christ, to learn to respond like Christ, to grow in grace and live by faith in Christ. Anger grieves the heart of a tender-hearted believer and drives him to thirst for righteousness, forgiveness, and strength that can be found only in Christ. The abusive person described in this publication is not so. He is not simply a man who struggles with angry outbursts now and then. Rather, he is a man who has practiced, justified, rationalized, and excused anger to such a degree that when aroused, he has become as dangerous as a cobra in a baby's nursery, or as the armed and angry criminal who roams free on our streets.

Many might ask, "Isn't some anger justified and righteous?" While it is agreed Scripture allows for the existence of righteous anger, the vast majority of expressed anger is clearly sinful. The most distinguishing mark of righteous anger is that it is *never* held or expressed *on behalf of oneself,* but only *on behalf of others* who cannot protect or care for themselves when mistreated., and then, only in a manner which itself is not sinful.

At the same time it is helpful to bear in mind King David's inspired commandment in Psalm 37:1 and 8. The Hebrew verb "charah" in verse 1 can be translated "fret", but also can properly be translated "to burn with anger" or, "be wrathful" or "inflame yourself". This then clarifies the focus of the commandment to, "Do not burn with anger because of evildoers." Similarly, in verse 8, the same verb can be read "Do not burn with anger, it leads only to evildoing." But this immediately raises the very serious question, "What should be my response to evil doers?"

The answer has two parts. First, we should respond with godly sorrow over all perpetrated evil, beginning with Christ's example. Isaiah 53:3; Luke 19:41; Romans 12:15-21 also apply. Secondly it is incumbent upon us to remember that when we are angry, our learning curve goes flat (Proverbs 19:19), and as a result, when we are angry we become part of the problem instead of being part of the godly solution. Ephesians 4:31 calls us to recognize our duty to, "put away all anger …", and James, the Lord's half-brother, flatly declares that, "the anger of man does not achieve the righteousness of God." (James 1:20).

The abusive man does not serve or protect his wife. Rather, he uses his wife for his own pleasure and purposes. Unlike Christ who sacrifices Himself to meet the legitimate needs of others, the abusive person sacrifices the reputation and welfare of others to satisfy his illegitimate and selfish desires. Thus, his anger is not on behalf of others, but out of extreme unhappiness when others fail to meet his perceived "needs," which are nothing more than his own selfish desires. Almost all rage and anger directed towards others begins with extreme self-centeredness and pride. The abusive man is typically resentful and enraged when his spouse fails to cater to his fleshly expectations and assumptions of supposedly deserved benefits or obligations, or has failed to appreciate how wonderful he believes he is.

Arguably, resentful and seething anger against others is one of the most common expressions of unrestrained pride, *even if well hidden*. Prideful anger often manifests itself under the guise of impatient intolerance of the failings or imperfections of others, and may often be described by the politically correct secular word *frustration*. At the same time, the person who condemns others typically demands others be forbearing and even eagerly willing to pardon his own corruptions (if admitted). A lack of genuine love for others and an unwillingness to forgive as God forgives almost always fuels explosive anger. God gives wise insight into the common link between self-righteous anger and overwhelming pride by coupling the two together in numerous passages of Scripture (Proverbs 21:23-24; I Samuel 25:2-38; Proverbs 29:22-23).

Anger can be expressed in many ways other than blowing up or speaking hatefully. Quiet or self-controlled people can also be very angry people. In fact, it is not unusual for an extremely cruel and abusive husband to appear calm, quiet and reserved, particularly in situations when he is around others outside the home. He might even describe himself as a patient and longsuffering man, or point out his kind and quiet humanitarian acts as proof he is not an angry man. Such a person is so unaware of how thoroughly anger rules his heart that he is convinced he is a "good" man who is sometimes provoked to anger by others, rather than a sinful and angry man who is destroying others. Abused wives are often confused about this double-sided person they live with, and often come to believe what the abusive husband so often declares about himself, namely that he becomes outraged because of some external stress or frustration, not because he is an angry person. Neither he, nor she, fully understands the deceptive nature of anger, or the many subtle ways anger surfaces and expresses itself. Following are a variety of ways people express sinful anger, besides the more obvious variations of "blowing up."

- *Displacement—Taking it out on someone else, or yourself*

- *Internalization—Privately sulking, pitying self*

- *Denial—Denying that a problem with anger or resentment exists, avoiding dealing with problems, attempts to circumvent problems, imagining problems are too big or too complicated to solve*

- *Resorting to sarcasm, biting humor, excessive teasing, inconsiderate actions, and manipulative crying*

- *Exhibiting forgetfulness, physical manifestations (diseases induced by internal agitation and anger), and an excessive desire for control of others*

- *Attempting to "spiritualize" sinful anger as righteous anger*

- *Seeking revenge against real or imagined wrongs*

The sinful desires that fuel anger are attitudes of "I want," "I need," and "I deserve" (James 4:1–3). The problem lies within us, not in our circumstances without. God clearly informs us that anger originates in our corrupted human nature and is the outward manifestation of inward self-motivated desires. When the angry person does not get what he wants or believes he needs or deserves, in all probability he will express his extreme displeasure in one way or another. For this reason, anger can be described as an adult temper tantrum pitched when God and others are not giving us what we want and what we believe we deserve. Before an abusive husband will ever be able to replace anger with love and forgiveness, he must first come to grips with the fact that he believes something that is not true and sinfully desires something God has not granted to him. He must come to understand and believe that his anger cannot be conquered without humble submission to an Almighty God's sovereign right to do as He pleases in our lives, or to govern our lives according to His will as revealed in the Word of God.

The angry man behaves as though God has placed him on earth for the express purpose of pursuing his own happiness and self-fulfillment. He fails to understand that we have been created for God's good and righteous purposes, not our own, for the glory of God, and not our own glory. He arrogantly ignores the fact that not one of us has the power to withstand God or prevent God from doing whatsoever He pleases in the affairs of any, saved or lost. Instead, he is devoted to manipulating people and circumstances in his life to force them into fulfilling his demands and expectations. When the inevitable problems, failures, and inconveniences of life thwart his will, he is outraged. He never seems to recognize that God has sovereignly ordered him to live in an imperfect world and expects him to respond to it by submitting to God's ways and will, and not by asserting his own. Despite all his foolish anger, threatening, pouting, and manipulating, the problems and frustrations in his life will continue; and he will not be one iota more satisfied or happy, no matter how often he seems to get his own way. Furthermore, God's work will continue regardless, according to His own plan and purpose. God declares, *"I have made the earth, the man and the beast that are upon the ground, by my great power and by my outstretched arm, and have given it unto whom it seemed meet unto me"* (Jeremiah 27:5).

Like a raging fire, anger is fueled by several problems. Some of these are:

- *Lack of trust in God's mercy*

- *Fear of God's rejection*

- *Lack of knowledge and confidence in God's love and willingness to forgive*

- *Weak or nonexistent understanding and reverence for God's sovereignty*

- *Failure to obey God's commandments concerning anger*

- *Perfectionism (Desire to look and feel righteous on the basis of one's own assumed merit)*

- *Consuming preoccupation with self*

- *Lack of love for others*

- *Unwillingness to forgive or overlook the failures of others*

- *Habitually justifying anger*

- *Inability to properly interpret problems, situations, and the behavior of others in the light of Scripture*

- *Poor listening and communication skills*

- *Insufficient constructive outlets for energy*

- *Failure to properly manage physical needs for adequate rest, proper nutrition, and exercise*

UNDERSTANDING ANGER BIBLICALLY

Anger is one of the most common expressions of the reality of our fallen nature, and as such, it is correctable with God's grace and mercy available in Jesus Christ. If we refuse to accept the Biblical truth that our own anger is the product of our own sinful nature, we are vulnerable to being tempted by Satan to indulge the sin of anger ever more viciously and more self deceptively. In fact, blaming Satan for our outbursts of anger can be a seemingly wonderful way to shift blame to avoid the humble repentance necessary to effectually overcome this powerful sin.

Anger begins in the mind. Leviticus 19:17–18 is a helpful text, directing attention to the principle that hatred of another can take residence in one's heart. Hatred is most often expressed in grudging anger, burning resentment, or outright violent acts for the purpose of seeking revenge. Before an angry outburst can occur, there must first be angry thoughts to give impetus to outward words and actions. Anger is one of the first sins to appear after the fall when Cain murdered Abel. Remember that Jesus equated anger with murder Matthew 5:21-22.

Anger is to be conquered/mastered. In Proverbs 16:32 Solomon rightly indicates that being slow to anger is a high virtue, better than political might, clearly implying that our natural inclination to become angry quickly can be conquered (using the Biblical means God has given). Proverbs 25:28 indicates that control over one's spirit is a crucial mark of true maturity, and the absence of that grace leaves one vulnerable! However, controlling one's spirit is not at all the same dynamic as the secular notion of controlling (the sin of) anger. When anger is understood as a sin that must be repented of, confessed, hated, and replaced with humble forbearance, it is a sin that can be overcome.

Anger rarely is God's will, and is not blessed of God. James 1:19 eloquently refutes any suggestion that anger is an instrument God blesses in accomplishing his will. A "cool spirit" is of immense value in times of crisis, but a hot-tempered man is always a curse to those around him (Proverbs 22:24–25).

Anger is a work of the flesh, the mark of an immature believer. James 3:13 presents a succinct and lovely contrast to the sin of anger, namely, "his works with meekness (gentleness) of wisdom." Anger is always violent, even if the violence is limited to verbal violence, but the angry person would do well to remember that *"Death and life are in the power of the tongue"* (Proverbs 18:21a). See also Proverbs 14:17; James 3:13; Galatians 5:19.

Sinful anger is a result of our pride and self-will. In Proverbs 29:22 Solomon reminds us that an angry, hot-tempered man will abound in transgressions—a sure evidence of the sin of unchecked pride. With the humility that engenders wisdom, comes the will and desire to turn from anger (Proverbs 29:8). When men self-destruct (cf. Proverbs 16:5, 18 and 29:23) pride is always at the root of that destruction, which usually occurs in the context of unchecked anger. Intense anger with others is also a dead giveaway of having an exalted opinion of oneself, forgetting that we deserve the wrath and curse of God for our sins, including death and the miseries of hell for eternity. Christ's sobering parable about the forgiven debt is a solemn warning not to forget our great debt before God when we are tempted to be unjustifiably angry with a fellow sinner (Matthew 18:21–35). James 4:1–10 is helpful in thinking about the connection of anger and selfish pride. Proverbs 14:17 indicates that a quick-tempered man is "foolish"—not a mark of a regenerated heart. Galatians 5:20 includes outbursts of anger as a "deed of the flesh"—a serious sin indicative of a very immature heart, if not an unsaved heart.

Anger influences others and destroys the atmosphere of a home. An angry spirit, indulged in without repentance can contaminate a whole household—and a single family member can actually exercise that corrupting power (Proverbs 21:19 and 15:17–18). Proverbs 22:24–25 so clearly indicates the corrupting nature of exhibited anger, as does Ephesians 6:4. Anger is like dynamite—it has enormous potential for destruction even in "small" quantities.

Anger is overcome with its opposite: love and forgiveness. Overcoming a so powerfully life dominating sin as habituated anger *must* be accomplished in the grace and power of God, grounded on Scripture. Anger must be replaced with the godly qualities of humility, joy, peace, thankfulness, love, forgiveness, and forbearance (Philippians 4:4–8; Psalm 37:7–10; Colossians 3:1–17; Proverbs 15:1; Psalm 37:8; Colossians 3:8).

Because anger is such a central issue, and a significant sin problem in virtually all abusive situations, we believe that taking the time to define anger is important in dealing Biblically with spousal abuse.

Anger: A Proposed Definition

1.   *A combination of emotion and a state of mind in which an individual elects to indulge in (expressed or hidden) the passion of wrath, or even fury, against one or more individuals and/or institutions and/or ideas which they choose to believe have negatively affected them, robbed them of one or more real or presumed "rights," have "hurt" them (in their prideful emotion and/or self-pity) and therefore legitimized a revengeful response against such individuals in one or more ways. In the grip of anger, such issues as the accuracy and*

truthfulness of their assumptions about another person become
essentially irrelevant to them.

2. *A strong feeling excited by real or supposed injury often*
   accompanied by a desire to take vengeance, or to obtain
   satisfaction from the offending party (Webster's New
   Universal Unabridged Dictionary)

3. *Synonyms: wrath, ire, irritation, indignation, resentment,*
   rage, fury.

FEAR

A fourth major contributor to wife abuse is a husband's unbelief and doubt concerning God's love for him, a fear of not having his emotional and other needs met by his spouse, a fear of failure, and a fear of being exposed for what he truly is—a weak, frail, fallible sinner just like all the rest of us. Emotional and social insecurity is part of that fearfulness.

Frantic, manipulative behavior generally comes from a fear of losing control over a person, or losing the person altogether. People who are controlling very often irrationally fear abandonment or rejection by a loved one. They do not understand that the more frantically they cling to a person and smother them with possessiveness, the more that person is going to sense that they are "trapped" and want to escape. Controlling people instinctively sense this resistance, and try to control so powerfully that the person who feels trapped will be unable to wiggle out of the encircling, controlling, and smothering management of their lives. A controlling spouse will usually violently react to any attempt a wife makes to escape his control or any attempt to act autonomously or in conflict to his desire.

Controlling people are fearful of losing their reputation. Consequently, they will often go to great lengths to put up a good front outside the home, while engaging in (sometimes) physically or mentally cruel acts of demeaning or controlling behavior behind closed doors. Fears of rejection, fears of being found out, or fears of losing the respect of others sometimes lead to fears that people are plotting against him, talking about him, or seeking to destroy him in some way. He may have a frantic fear that his wife is sharing information that puts him in a bad light or have a fear of counseling, especially by a pastor before whom he does not want to lose face. Some abusive husbands have come to the place where they sincerely recognize their misery and their serious problem with violence and anger, but are so afraid of being rejected, they cannot bring themselves to seek the help of even the most compassionate and competent counselor. Such men often suffer in torment for years only to end up being forced to submit to court ordered counseling after being arrested for domestic violence or assault and battery. Sadly, the shock, humiliation, and expense of an arrest is sometimes the only way the abuser's fear and pride are broken down enough to enable him to face the problem for what it truly is.

Fear of exposure unsurprisingly leads the abusive man to persist in deceitful cover-ups that can become quite elaborate. He will change or falsify facts for his own purpose or profit without hesitation, and will resort to artful management of others by shrewdly using influence with others in an unfair or fraudulent way. His skill at manipulation can become so refined that he rivals an experienced con artist in his ability to sway opinion or control other people's actions or thinking for his own purposes or gratification. Over the years, he tragically has used his best intellectual and emotional and social energies and endowments to hone his refined skills as a master manipulator. He uses his manipulative skills to insure secrecy, continue in his behavior, get what he wants, or disguise his intentions, fears, and failures.

To counteract fears of inadequacy, an abuser desires to feel powerful and exalted over his wife, even as her spirit is broken by the abusive behavior. This controlling power can take form in a variety of abuses, including sexual perversions in which the husband demands his wife submit to humiliating demands, or participate in demeaning or painful sexual relations. It is not at all uncommon for abusive men to force their wives to do that which by right a husband has no legitimate privilege from God to require, usually in the secrecy of their own homes or bedrooms. As the woman is forced into submission and her spirit is crushed by her husband's anger and ridicule, the abusive man is exhilarated by his rush of power over her, and is temporarily satisfied that he is in absolute control of his wife. What he does not recognize is that he has bought into a delusion, and is far from being in control. In reality, he has been seduced by his own sinful lusts, by his own sinful thinking, and the lie of the devil. Such abusers are, in fact, controlled by evil and, if unrepentant, are being incrementally brought under the dominance and power of Satan himself.

Behavior such as this is just one example of the fear-driven man's determination to break the wife's spirit, which is the overall purpose of abuse, both mental and physical. It is a means of illegitimately exalting oneself over ones wife to avoid experiencing a sense of inferiority or being confronted by the truth, no matter how kindly or humbly his wife may seek to communicate that truth. In many cases, an abusing husband may secretly desire that his wife lose any sense of reasonable intellectual ability. He may suggest, either subtly or overtly, that she is unstable, mentally or spiritually sick, or stupid. If this continues, it is not uncommon for an abused wife to begin believing she has no ability to form lasting friendships, to cook, to care for her own children, to respond to her husband's needs in a Biblical way, to pursue personal interests, or think accurately about anything. A controlling husband interprets this helplessness and passivity as appropriate submission on her part. Sadly, it is a terribly sinful way of dealing with his fears of inadequacy or fears of his wife challenging or leaving him.

Abusive men are almost always fearful of their wife excelling in any area of life in which they want to excel or remain "superior." They do not tolerate competition well, even though they wrongly interpret any success on the wife's part as competition. Typically, they are terrified to admit their wife could do anything as well, or better than they can. To commend or acknowledge anything achieved by their spouse is viewed as a threat to the insecure abuser. He might brag about his wife's achievements in front of people, only to privately pick apart and criticize her interests or accomplishments in the privacy of the home. Again, this nitpicking and fault finding is a means of bolstering a sagging ego and gaining a sense of superiority over his wife.

It is not uncommon for abusive husbands to seek "affirmation" and attention from other women to assuage their nagging fears. Such men often gravitate towards careers where they can legitimately control others and elicit admiration from women. This can lead to adultery, but commonly is manifested in indulgence in sexual fantasies, pornographic perversions, or seductive behavior. An abusive man can himself be openly charming and flirtatious with other women, yet be incensed and disgusted if his wife is openly charming *without* being flirtatious, or if anyone complains about his questionable behavior.

Jealousy as an Expression of Fear
Fear leads to jealousies of many kinds, and is an almost universal characteristic of an abusive man. He may imagine his wife has a boyfriend, or boyfriends, and will go to extremes in his attempts to verbally pressure her into admitting to some kind of immorality. His suspicions can range from mild to severe and can become an overwhelming obsession to the point where he will accuse his wife of flirting when there is absolutely no evidence of her doing so. A wife can become so fearful of triggering her husband's wild suspicions and accusations that she fears shaking a man's hand, looking a man in the eyes, or speaking to a salesman. Many women have described screaming sessions where the enraged husband forces her to stay in a room for hours while he screams in her face

and demands she admit to indiscretion with another man.

Other women describe husbands who seem to "explode" short-ly after marriage, or on their honeymoon. Typically, the husband will demand that his new wife describe in detail every boyfriend she has ever had and every physical or sexual act that took place from the time of her childhood. Later, he will bring up names of past boyfriends, remind her of her indiscretions and sins, accuse her of still seeing or wanting a past boyfriend or imagining she is still in contact with someone from her past. He mentally relives any description he has extracted from her until his thoughts of her with another man trigger rage and disgust and give him an excuse to remind her she is a "tramp" and "whore" and a "rebellious" and "despicable" person. He thus feels justified in humiliating his wife with cruel verbal attacks that demoralize her and chip away her confidence in her God-given ability to identify truth and sense God's forgiveness or God's direction for her life.

The abuser's jealousy often extends beyond jealousy of other men and exhibits itself as jealousy of family members, or even of his own children. Many battered women have described terrify-ing abuse that began during their first pregnancy or shortly after the child's birth. Still other abusers manifest jealousy, fear, and resentment of things other than people or relationships. Many are insanely jealous of their wife's character or spiritual life. In fact, the godlier some wives are, the more their abusive husbands try to tempt them to behave sinfully to be able to critically belittle their Christian testimony. Or, he may be hyper-vigilant in watching for any kind of failure on her part to point it out and prove she isn't so spiritual, or is self-righteous. This kind of jealousy may lead to accusations that his wife is "going to church too much," or "being taken advantage of at church," or "too involved with people at church." The jealous husband may act as if God were his competition, and is to blame for his wife's seeming lack of attention toward him. This kind of reasoning is commonly attached to anyone the wife enjoys or has a relationship with, including her family. The fearful, jealous husband sees these relationships as a threat to his dominance, and he will work relentlessly to keep his wife from cultivating or enjoying a relationship with anyone other than himself, even if that relationship is with God!

The Root of Fear

Ultimately, the root cause of ALL ungodly fear is the sin of unbelief. Quite simply, it is the unwillingness to take God at His Word, the unwillingness to believe that He will bless those who trust in Him and the unwillingness to believe or trust in God's loving care over His children (See Proverbs 3:21–16; Matthew 6:24–36; 19:23). Such excessive fear may also be a clear indicator or "red flag" that a man has never been converted and is not a child of God. In this spiritual condition, the wrath of God abides on him, and fear is a natural result. The only remedy for the fear of God's real and impending judgment is repentance toward God and faith toward the Lord Jesus Christ. The Scriptures plainly teach that the Holy Spirit *"convinces the world of sin, of righteousness, and of judgment to come"* (John 16:8–9). Thus, the unconverted man may inwardly be convinced he is a sinner heading for judgment, yet not be able (or willing) to identify the source of his fear except the Lord reveal it to him. In his resistance and rebellion towards God's Spirit, he wrongly blames his wife or others for the torments of his fear.

To understand *fear* in the Biblical sense of the word, we need to remember that this word, like many other words addressed in the Bible, is not well understood today. We are a society that does not deal well with the subject of fear. *Fear* is a word that often strikes apprehension in our hearts. Even in Bible-believing churches, our understanding of the Biblical truths concerning fear is often pitifully weak. There is, of course, a proper fear of God, which is life giving, therapeutic, restorative, and maturing (Proverbs 1:7). This fear is not to be understood as terror, in the abject, or cowardly sense, but rather in the sense of a profound, reverential, and loving awe and humble realization that the power and justice of God is such that we could be consumed in a moment but for His grace, and that He is a God not to be trifled with, and certainly not to be dealt with as a celestial "pal." The fear of God produces an awareness of God's presence and certain accountability, as well as deep gratitude and worship toward God. The Scriptures tell us, "by the fear of the Lord men depart from evil," and "the fear of the Lord is the beginning of wisdom." The fear of Lord is further defined as hating evil (Proverbs 8:13), as being satisfying (Proverbs 14:27), and as having the power to change or sanctify believers (Proverbs 14:27). The fear of the Lord, therefore, is crucial to experiencing a right relationship with God or appropriating truth. We develop a fear of God as we recognize God's majesty (Jeremiah 10:7), holiness (Revelation 15:4), forgiveness (Psalm 130:4), goodness (1 Samuel 12:24), and righteous judgment against sin (Revelation 14:7).

In contrast to the fear of the Lord, which characterizes a person who is submitting to and being controlled by God's Spirit, the *fear of man* characterizes the person who is being controlled by his own reasoning and will. The fear of man can be described as "any anxiety that is caused by real or imagined discomfort, rejection, or danger being imposed by another human being." The Scriptures tell us that the origins of the fear of man are many, including uncertainty or unbelief (2 Corinthians 11:3), impending judgment (Hebrews 11:7), persecution (John 20:19), events of nature (Acts 27:17, 29), disobedience (Genesis 3:10), suspicion (Acts 9:26), final events (Luke 21:26), or impending death (Hebrews 2:15). Some of the effects the fear of man has on a Christian include demoralization (1 Samuel 13:5–8), paralysis (Matthew 28:4), and a silent testimony (John 9:22). One thing is certain— to the degree one manifests a fear of man, he will not fear God, and to the degree one fears God, he will not fear man.

The Scriptures further teach us that the fear of man, or absence of a fear of God, produces unreasonable fears. "The wicked flee when no man pursueth," is just one example found in Proverbs 28:1. Fears of unpleasant or threatening circumstantial possibilities, or of the ability and presumed certainty of enemies harming us (while having, at times, some measure of truth) is often more a state of mind than a fact. It is interesting and significant that even unregenerate observers of the human condition have noted that about 90 percent of what we fear generally never comes to pass.

Or, as it has been put in colloquial terms, "Most of the bridges we fear to cross aren't even there." Our human minds have a great ability to pessimistically sense, and then enlarge upon, possible disasters. Focusing upon them becomes an end in itself which can paralyze an effective response to such fears. This kind of paralyzing concentration on fear always goes hand in hand with the failure to know and understand the application of God's promises to His children, a failure to understand and trust in His loving fatherly care and concern for them, and a failure to cultivate a proper fear of God.

There are many passages of Scripture that are helpful in the development of proper trust in God. Psalms 91 and 23 are excellent chapters to study and ponder. Verses such as, "He will shelter you under the shadow of his wings. A thousand shall fall at thy side and ten thousand at thy right hand, but it shall not come nigh thee . . ." and, "Yea though I walk through the valley of the shadow of death, I will fear no evil for thou art with me . . ." are examples of the kind of remarkable care that God declares He has extended towards those who trust Him. It is incumbent upon us to believe our Savior's assurances, because the failure to do so constitutes a rejection of God's self-declaration of His faithfulness and shepherding care. The Christian who rightly understands the providential care of God, understands that God has sovereignly and unilaterally declared His supernatural shepherding as an intrinsic part of salvation, and hence our sanctification (2 Thessalonians 2:13). The more one begins to appropriate these truths, the more he is freed from the paralyzing and tormenting fears of man. Likewise, the less one understands and appropriates these truths, the less one is able to conquer fears and insecurities.

Christ told us not to be anxious about tomorrow, about what clothing we would wear or about what we would eat (Matthew 6:25–34). This warning (in the form of a commandment) can be obeyed by realizing and understanding that God's providential care is phenomenally sufficient and extends beyond our power to comprehend it fully or even in some scientific sense. We can but feebly grasp fully God's ability to feed every sparrow and to clothe every flower of the field. And yet, here is an assertion of Jesus Christ that brings joy to the believing heart, even while it provokes the unbelieving to explain it away or spiritualize it to the point of making it less than the promise it is. The net effect of such a response puts Christ in the position of being a liar, no matter how pious our language, and that is something no tenderhearted believer would ever want to do. Additionally, this response constitutes the sin of unbelief, not just with respect to salvation, but also with respect to the character and nature of God and His declared intimate involvement in the life and welfare of every true believer.

Hence, an abusive husband is essentially saying, "I don't believe God's grace is sufficient to enable me to live with my wife on God's terms, and be blessed, and have my needs met." Such a husband is determined to satisfy his own perceived desires on his own terms, by his own perverted means, and as a result, suffers all the consequences of the fears he is powerless to absolve, no matter how much or how hard he tries to do so. One of the marks of fear is always the fleshly endeavor to provide a corrupted form of security that presumably will compensate for the arena in which the fear is exhibited. The humble believer who sees God not only as Savior, but as Heavenly Father, Good Shepherd, and sanctifier of His people, does not have to manipulate others to have a sense of confidence that his own needs will be met in a way that is both fulfilling and consistent with God's Holy Word.

4

QUESTIONS ABUSED WIVES COMMONLY ASK

Question: *I realize I'm in danger, and I want to do something about my situation immediately. What do I do now?*

Answer: A critically important first step toward resolving abuse comes when a wife faces the fact that, for all her husband's manipulative efforts, somewhere she must honestly and humbly admit that: (a) there is a problem, (b) it is severe, (c) it is not just hers, (d) she is unable to handle it herself, and (e) she is not in sin because she has faced the unpleasant truth about her husband.

Once an abused wife recognizes the abuse for what it is, she must determine to respond in a godly manner. By godly we mean in a manner consistent with Biblical principles, free from hatefulness, paralyzing fear, or vindictiveness. Remember, it is NOT godly to be passive and do nothing! It IS godly to actively overcome evil with good, which may include reporting criminal abuse to proper authorities or separating yourself from your husband until he is able to accept responsibility for his destructive behavior and has learned how to live with you without resorting to the kind of thinking and responding that has made him vulnerable to using abusive speech or violence against you or the children. Your first godly response should be to prayerfully find a counselor or pastor who is able to help you determine the safest way to intervene and deal with your husband. (See Appendix A for further help with this need.) Following are five things to remember that will help you as you learn to deal Biblically with an abusive husband.

C *ry to the Lord.*

L *ean on Christ for mercy, grace, help.*

A *ct Biblically. (Overcome evil with good. Use God-given resources.)*

S *peak softly, but truthfully.*

H *arbor no grudge—don't retaliate.*

Question: *I didn't know my husband had a temper or could become violent until he flew into a rage and hit me on our honeymoon. I have felt like a failure as a wife, but I can't seem to make him happy or do things right. We've now been married five years and we have three children, but he has only gotten angrier and more violent since I don't have as much time to do what he wants with three small children to take care of. Last week my husband broke my jaw, but he convinced me to lie to the doctors who examined me in the emergency room. I told them I ran into a wall.*

I've finally come to a point where I realize my husband has a problem and needs help, but I'm afraid to involve anyone in our life. My husband already has a difficult time paying bills and surviving on his job so I hate to add one more stress to his life. I love my husband and want to do the right thing. What should I do?

Answer: Understanding several simple, Biblical principles will encourage a wife who is contemplating what direction she should take. One is that it takes more love to confront a problem than to avoid it by denial, or inaction, or some other manipulative means. Initially there may be more short-term pain when exposure and confrontation takes place. However, Scripture speaks very clearly regarding this concern again and again. For instance, we read in Proverbs 27:6, "Faithful are the wounds of a friend, but the kisses of an enemy are deceitful." And in Ephesians 4:25, "Wherefore, putting away lying, speak every man truth with his neighbor: for we are members one of another." If we really believe our husband should be our best friend and that he is our closest neighbor, these commandments apply. Ephesians 5:11 instructs us "do not participate the unfruitful deeds of darkness, but instead even expose them".

Another principle to be remembered is that sin is never static. Sin begets sin. The longer a problem is unaddressed and uncorrected, the worse it becomes. The wife who hopes for some miraculous intervention, apart from the means of God's ordinary promises and Biblical truth to lift the problem out of her hands, probably hopes in vain. God has clearly indicated that it is her responsibility in her office of a helper, suitable to her husband, to actively confront a problem, not passively ignore it. She married him for better or for worse. Confronting the situation in order to resolve it is some of the "worse" as opposed to the "better." Dealing with the "worse" includes the commitment to love a husband enough to get him the help that he needs, even if doing so is personally and emotionally difficult, even if it is humiliating or frightening.

Question: *I am married to a man that often threatens to strangle me. On one occasion, he had his hands around my neck so tightly that I passed out. I thought for sure he was going to kill me. I know I need to find shelter in a safe place and let my pastor confront my husband, but I am afraid of what my husband will do. He has said that if I ever told anyone, he'd make life so miserable on me I'd wish I hadn't. He's threatened to divorce me if I left him, and has said I wouldn't get one dime from him in support. I know he couldn't afford to support both of us if we were living separately. What should I do?*

Answer: First, you need to understand that any husband who puts his hands around your neck so tightly that you pass out is one small step away from murdering you. One day he might very well become so enraged he squeezes your neck a little too long and a little too tightly. You are not being longsuffering by allowing this to continue. Rather, you are putting your life at risk, your husband in danger of spending the rest of his life in prison and your children in danger of growing up without mother or father for the rest of their lives. It's not worth the risk.

If, as a wife, you fear being unable to support yourself if your husband is exposed and you are separated for a season to the point where you are paralyzed in your decision-making, you must realize you have chosen a very deadly and dangerous way of thinking. Such a response amounts to continuing to support your husband's dynamic sin. The rebuke of Christ in Matthew 6:5–34 concerning anxiety over tomorrow certainly applies here. A wife with several small children may think, "That's easy for you to say while writing this, but I have five little ones and no marketable job skills. What can I do?" For those who have taken seriously what we have said in this publication, namely that God must be at the center of any solution that lasts and works, this aspect is no exception. For believers, help can be sought from the ministry of vibrant, Bible-believing congregations. For those with no church connections, there are sound welfare agencies, which can sometimes be tapped for assistance.

To begin with, ponder the statement that he'd "make life so miserable for me I'd wish he hadn't." My friend, he has already done that! That threat is empty, because the reason you need to get shelter is that he IS making life "so miserable!" Here is an example of precisely where the visible church is obligated to assist a godly wife with diaconal mercy (ministry of mercy overseen by deacons) if the husband refuses to adequately support her. (Incidentally, refusing to support a wife is often one of the marks of an abusive husband who is in the stages of abuse where he begins to escalate the "pressure" on his wife when he senses she is considering leaving.) When a wife caves in to such threats she is basically saying she is unwilling to trust her Heavenly Father, or to submit to God's way of doing the work of His kingdom.

If you wish to have assistance of any kind, you must be willing to discuss the problem honestly with whomever you go to for help. If pride keeps you from doing this, then truly here is a case where you want the benefit without the cost. Humbling ourselves to admit that there is a serious problem which we cannot handle all by ourselves (Luke 12:26, John 15:5c) is always a central factor in seeing God's mighty hand of sovereign grace resolving situations that we cannot resolve in our flesh and in our own strength (Matthew 23:12; Luke 14:11; Hebrews 4:14–16).

Question: *Should I confront my husband by myself?*
Answer: If you believe you are an abused wife in any kind of danger, you must NOT confront the problem alone. Attempting to confront an abusive husband about the seriousness of his sin is like attempting to confront a dangerous criminal about his crime. In both cases, you need protection and the added experience of people who can help you.

If you are an abused wife and you have already made several attempts to lovingly hold your husband responsible for his behavior, you must not confront the problem alone again. There are many reasons for this. First, the Bible clearly teaches that a Christian who is wronged by another should involve a third party when the offender refuses to recognize his sin or repent. An abused wife tends to stop at the first level of confrontation early in the marriage, and goes no further in involving others for fear of retaliation from her husband. Abused wives discover very quickly that none of their attempts to reason with their husbands or appeal to their need for repentance succeeds to bring about any lasting change. To continue trying to confront the problem alone will not only put a wife in danger, but will tend to increase anger and an unwillingness to cooperate. At this point, many wives try to minimize the problem in their own mind and attempt to explain away the husband's obviously dangerous behavior. They might resort to ignoring him, appeasing him, or trying to "out manipulate" him. Such women must realize these tactics never result in a successful resolution of the problems and sins that underlie abuse. The only hope for change is a husband's repentance toward God and subsequent growth in grace (sanctification). The action God calls for in cases where an offender will not respond to a loving confrontation is to involve a qualified third party, and then involve the church body if necessary.

Women who ignore this Biblical safeguard and means of assistance and try to deal with the situation alone continue to be candidates for manipulation by somebody who has worked for years at learning how he can manipulate his wife. Remember that he is a master at it—you are not. Better to involve a person who is understanding and skillful in responding to abusive men.

Question: *To whom do I go to for help?*

Answer: You must choose the person from whom you are seeking help with great care. Sadly, it is not uncommon for well-intentioned and caring Christians who are not familiar with the nature and sinful dynamics of abuse to advise a wife to go back and be more submissive, more loving, more kind, and more giving. The counselor may suggest that if a wife will accept a deeper level of subservience and capitulation to the demands of her husband and if she will continue to try every possible means to seek reconciliation, that this will provide a breakthrough in his destructive behavior. The genuinely abused wife does well to remember that in the United States of America, there have been numerous cases in the last fifty years in which well-intentioned pastors urged abused wives to go back to their husbands and be "nicer"—which ultimately led to the wife being murdered or permanently maimed.

Well-meaning friends and counselors often lead women to either under-react (he won't hurt you if you are submissive), over-react (you need to divorce him), or improperly react (you probably provoke him) to be abusive. You must seek competent Biblical counsel from someone who can help you be objective, and help you respond appropriately in your particular situation. Finding such help may be very difficult. Competent Biblical counselors who will not mix Biblical truth with popular secular notions are not that numerous although, thankfully, their numbers are growing.

Question: *I have gone to my pastor several times when my husband has gone out of control and threatened me. I've tried to explain how afraid I am and how concerned I am for our little son who is terrified when his daddy begins to scream and push me around. Recently he blew up when I forgot to cook what he wanted for dinner and got so mad he threw the food across the room, shoved me to the floor, kicked me in my stomach several times, and then grabbed our son and drove off in the car at high speed. Our son was terrified and sobbing when he finally returned home, but my husband would not allow me to put him to bed or comfort him. When I explained what happened to my pastor, and told him I wanted to live with my parents until my husband could be trusted not to abuse me or our son, he told me I would be sinning if I left my husband. He believes I'm exaggerating the situation and explained that since my life isn't in danger, it's wrong to* *leave. He suggested I learn to be more forgiving and more sensitive to my husband's needs. How do I respond?*

Answer: A woman living in such a volatile and dangerous situation ought to be able to confidently seek the help of her church or pastor. Sadly, oftentimes abused wives may not be understood when they do so. In such cases, a woman ought not to panic if the first time she addresses her problems with her pastor he thinks that she is just exaggerating the difficulty, or that she is angling for divorce.

A wife must state to her pastor carefully, humbly, and repeatedly, "I do not want to divorce, that is not my purpose. I am committed to reconciliation but realize that our particular problem is one that perhaps cannot be solved when we are together. My husband's facade of niceness and charm is such that those who do not know what goes on at home understandably may not initially grasp the nature and extent of the abuse the children and I have endured. Yet it must be addressed, and the children's safety and my own safety must take precedence now." If her pastor refuses to heed such a carefully qualified plea for Biblically structured safety and reconciliation, then a truly abused wife should seek help elsewhere.

Question: *My husband has always been abusive, but lately he's begun scaring me by making me sit on the floor naked while he holds a gun to my head and yells at me to tell him who I was sleeping with. I've never even looked at another man, but my husband has accused me of having boyfriends ever since we were married. Nothing I say convinces him I am not cheating on him. He continues to call me hor-*

rible names and accuse me, and sometimes he beats me and threatens to kill me or the kids. He's started carrying a loaded gun and keeps it on his bedside table even though I beg him to put it away where the children won't find it. I'm really scared and I want help, but I don't know where to go. I know if he finds me, he'll hurt me or one of the kids. He's told me hundreds of times he would kill me if I ever tried to leave him. A restraining order wouldn't stop him if he were in a rage. I finally got enough courage to call our pastor, but he said I needed to find someone more competent to help me. I have no family or friends that I could live with temporarily, so he suggested I call a shelter for battered women. He's agreed to find an experienced pastor to help him talk to my husband, but wants me to go to a shelter so I am in a safe place when my husband finds out I want a separation. I called the police department to get the name of a shelter but I haven't called any of the numbers they gave me yet. What should I do?

Answer: At that most difficult point in time in which the wife makes the decision that she must act, the question of where to go becomes critical. Ideally, it is helpful for an abused woman to live with another Christian family outside her area that is not known to the husband or children. Sometimes a pastor will arrange this with another pastor in a different city. When this kind of arrangement isn't possible and there are no other resources immediately available, a shelter is sometimes the best alternative for a woman who is in danger. (See Appendix B for information on shelters for battered women.) Most shelters who offer the highest level of protection will not allow you to bring your car or a cell phone that may have tracking capability. This is for your protection and the protection of those you stay with.

Question: *My husband is extremely angry and abusive, even around our children, but he never actually hits me. Is this wife abuse?*

Answer: Many abusive husbands are concerned enough with their reputation that they consciously hold themselves "in check" when their rage becomes dangerous. Or, they may spend increasing amounts of time working (or playing) away from home as a means of controlling their explosive outbursts. A godly wife and mother needs to understand that children, raised in this kind of secretive cruelty and hypocrisy, are not only severely scarred by such a home life, but have great potential to rebel against both parents in years to come, or become spouse abusers themselves. Quite simply, we are never free to ignore the requirement to resist evil, and to overcome evil with good. Do not passively assume doing nothing is better than going through the disruption of getting help, even in cases where it appears a husband can control the extent of his hostility and violence.

Question: *I believe if I could just learn how to explain things better to my husband, he would understand how much he hurts me and change. Can you tell me how to make my husband understand?*

Answer: Do not engage in repeated attempts to "make" your husband understand. First of all, you do not possess the power or ability to "make him" understand or think anything! Besides this, he is most likely adamantly unwilling to view your distress from your perspective, and does not consider your feelings valid. Your explaining, pleading, and describing, no matter how intense or sincere, will not accomplish a change of heart in your husband.

Question: *When my husband gets in my face and starts yelling and screaming at the top of his lungs, I usually start crying and pleading* *for him to listen to me and stop. Should I yell back at him instead?*

Answer: The moment your husband begins a verbal tirade, ask him to stop, and remove yourself from his presence as quickly as possible before it escalates. Do not cry, scream, or retaliate when your husband is in a rage. This will only fuel his anger further, give him a "justification" for striking you, and possibly put you in great physical danger.

Question: *What do I do when my husband starts picking a fight and twisting everything I say?*

Answer: Make your appeals to your husband when he is calm, not when he is hostile and agitated. Stick to simple requests and statements, and do not allow yourself to be diverted when he counters your requests with personal attacks, changes the subject, or makes sarcastic remarks. Rather than engaging in an argument (which you cannot win) or defending yourself, restate your statement, question, or suggestion calmly and deliberately.

Before your husband will admit wrong to you, he will most likely twist your efforts for a Biblical confrontation into a verbal attack on you. Do not respond to this tactic by defending yourself or retaliating! Stick to whatever you expressed was wrong, but drop the discussion as quickly as possible. Always remember that short, simple statements are better than long, drawn-out explanations.

Before speaking to him, be sure to spend time in prayer, specifically asking God to give you appropriate words and your husband a listening heart.

Question: *Isn't separation an overly disruptive means of correcting the problem? Is there a way to deal with the problem without separating?*

Answer: If correcting the problem requires a period of physical separation until the husband has not only admitted his sin, but received real help in overcoming it, is that not a small price to pay for the long-term restoration of the marriage, protection of the family, and possibly the salvation of his soul? "A prudent (wise) man foreseeth the evil, and hideth himself: but the simple (foolish) pass on, and are punished" (Proverbs 22:3).

Question: *I often feel like I hate my husband when he berates me and pushes me around, but I don't want to divorce him. Will scaring him by threatening to divorce him or separate from him help him know how I feel when he rejects me and make him more serious about changing?*

Answer: If you expect God to bless your efforts, you must take every needed step in redemptive love. Never must the motive of revenge or retribution be allowed a moment's lodging in your heart. Your first goal must be the honor of Jesus Christ and obedience to His holy word. Although separation may be necessary, to try to SCARE him with the threat of divorce is not biblical. You must not use any kind of manipulation to win your husband. Your job is to speak the truth with love (Ephesians 4:15-16). It is God who can change your husband's heart. Seek to handle injustice His way!

Question: *My husband gave me a concussion by repeatedly banging* *my head into the wall. I was able to call 911 for help. The officers arrested my husband but he was released on bail a few hours later. Even though I got a restraining order, I didn't trust him not to break into the house and hurt me so I went to a shelter with my baby. My pastor talked to my husband and subsequently he admitted he was wrong and wants to change. I want to go back home and give my husband another chance, but my pastor wants me to wait until my husband demonstrates a true willingness to submit to counseling and demonstrates he has acquired sufficient knowledge about his sinful anger and how it is conquered. My husband has promised me he will continue counseling if I come home immediately. I believe he is sincere about getting help. Should I continue the separation or go back home?*

Answer: Because many godly wives who have been abused still long for restoration of the marriage, you must humbly admit that you are the least objective participant in determining your husband's sincerity and repentance. Therefore, if separation is advised in order to protect your safety and the safety of your children, or to give your counselor the opportunity to intervene on your behalf, do not agree to live together with your husband until a third party, (i.e. a competent pastoral counselor), is truly satisfied that your husband has humbly accepted the counseling, has clearly acknowledged his sins, has plainly expressed repentance, has humbly sought forgiveness, and has demonstrated the fruits of true repentance for a reasonable period of time (Proverbs 9:7–10). If your husband has not acquired the necessary knowledge and ability to deal Biblically with his anger, coming home too soon will put both you and he at risk. When couples come back together too soon, the process of reconciliation is likely to end in failure, discouragement or a refusal to continue with the long-term counseling that is needed. You and your husband must both learn and practice the tools that will enable you to handle problems and replace abusive behavior with righteous behavior BEFORE you resume living together.

Question: *If I seek help or call the police without my husband's approval or permission, aren't I being an unsubmissive wife?*

Answer: Realize that there is more than one Biblical principle which applies in wife abuse situations. Yes, a wife is to submit to her husband, but never absolutely as if her husband were God. In fact, a husband's governing authority extends only so far as that rule is Biblical. Whenever any husband's arbitrary requirements of his wife contradict Scripture, that wife must obey the Word of God, and follow the normative example of Peter, James, and John when they said to the Sanhedrin (who had just given them an unbiblical command), "We must obey God rather than man." Additionally, all Christians, including godly wives, are to preserve life, not jeopardize it. Uncontrollable anger is the forerunner of murder. The proper response to a murderous rage is to immediately seek help from authorities God has provided to protect society from those who would harm them. It would be quite silly to ask a murderer for his permission to call the police or seek protection through church authority!

Since we now have so much documented evidence in regards to wife abuse, we know that there is a significant danger that such abuse, if unchecked and uncorrected, can, and very well may, lead to the murder or maiming of the wife and/or children. If your husband does physical harm to you, it is a crime, and should be handled as such. And remember, if he murders or maims you, he will be arrested and sentenced to spend many years in prison. In essence, your not dealing with the problem puts not only your life in jeopardy, but his life as well. Better to deal with the problem before he does something that will do irreparable damage to his own life as well as yours. If he ends up in prison for murder, he will weep many tears wishing you had done something drastic to help him and stop him before it culminated in such suffering and loss.

Question: *My husband occasionally becomes violent and slaps me around. Lately he's gotten more violent and has given me bruises and black eyes. I finally sought the help of a counselor when my husband went on a business trip. The counselor has advised me to separate from my husband until he is willing to accept appropriate Biblical counsel and make serious changes in his life. I want to follow this advice, but I'm afraid this is not Biblical. I do want to do the right thing and be a submissive and godly wife. Is separation a Biblical option?*

Answer: Paul prefaces the command to live peaceably with all men with two qualifying statements in Romans 12:18. He said, "If it be possible," which implies that sometimes it is not possible to live peaceably with someone. Second, he said, "as much as lieth in you," or, to the degree it depends on you, live peaceably. When it is not possible to live in peace with a spouse, Paul gives guidelines to a separation in 1 Corinthians 7:11, which is further evidence Paul understood there are unusual circumstances when a separation is necessary in cases such as spousal abuse. Proverbs 22:24-25 can help determine whether separation is necessary.

Godly wives will likely experience a predictable temptation to be fearful, namely, that if she exposes the abuse, or especially if she separates from her husband for a season for the purpose of safeguarding herself and the children, she is thereby disobeying God's clear and repeated commandment to wives to be in submission to (or submit to) their husbands. As with any passage of Scripture, no text should be looked at apart from other texts which bear on the same issue in principle. To begin with, only God demands absolute and unqualified obedience of any of His redeemed children, be they male or female (Matthew 28:19–20; John 14:15, 21, 23–24; 15:10, 14, 11; 5:3).

We are never to obey any evil instruction or commandment (Romans 12:9, 17, 21; Proverbs 17:13) even if that command comes from a husband, a pastor, elder, or deacon. So Peter and John told the Sanhedrin that they could not obey the Sanhedrin's (evil) order since it conflicted with God's greater authority and commandments (Acts 4:16–20). Consequently, a wife indeed is obligated to humbly and lovingly obey her husband, unless he requires of her one or more evil actions or attitudes (including the requirement to do nothing about his abusive treatment of her which clearly violates Ephesians 5:25–31).

Question: *Is there any hope that my husband can change and become a loving husband without repentance?*
Answer: It is possible, though unlikely, that your husband may learn to control violent behavior to some extent without recognition of his actions as sin, or without true repentance towards

God. This external change is what the world might call "behavior modification." Behavior modification without heart transformation is unacceptable to a Christian who understands the power of the Scriptures to transform lives, and knows that unless the heart is brought into conformity with the Word of God, no genuine change in intent or motivation has taken place. Men who learn to "control" their anger to some degree, do not conquer their anger.

Many abusers, once arrested and charged with a crime, fear being arrested again, resulting in an outward change of behavior. While fear may act as a deterrent to violent behavior, it does not change the heart. Court ordered anger management classes may teach a husband how to restrain or redirect anger so he doesn't repeat the crime of assault and battery, they do not teach him the necessity of repentance toward God and man. As a result, he learns to manage anger but does not conquer it. There will be no heart level change of behavior without seeking change on God's terms! Nor does a measure of self-control change an abuser's basic belief system which gives rise to the demoralizing and vicious verbal attacks on his wife. Yes, it is remotely possible for your husband to alter his violent behavior somewhat, even without repentance toward God. But no, it is not possible for your husband to ever conquer his anger, learn how to love as God defines love, or experience any kind of life-changing heart transformation without the God-given grace of repentance.

True Biblically grounded repentance, (as opposed to fleshly remorse, self-pity, and manipulative apologies to get out of a hot spot) must be understood as a God-given grace which cannot be self-generated (Hebrews 12:16–17) but is a gift of the Holy Spirit (2 Timothy 2:25). Psalm 51 is the incomparably best model of the true God-given grace of repentance, containing all the constituent elements of that crucial gift and work of God's Spirit. What does true repentance look like? Study 2 Corinthians 7:9-11. Time reveals whether repentance is genuine or a contrived act.

When John the Baptist came preaching a baptism of repentance, a crucial element in his instructive declaration was that true repentance must be validated by fruits of repentance. Fruit takes time to develop, and so do evidences of genuine repentance. Hence, while a wife can humanly say to her husband, "I forgive you," if he says, "I repent," and asks for her forgiveness (Luke 17:3–4), she is not obligated to assume that a genuine reformation of his abusive treatment of her has taken place without adequate, long-term, observable evidence supporting that (Matthew 7:15–20). Remember that God commands us to forgive, but nowhere in the Bible does God command us to trust another human being (Jeremiah 17:5). The limited trust we develop in human relationships is earned as character is revealed in day to day life.

Question: *Is it possible for women to be abusive in the same way as men?*

Answer: It is indeed possible for women to be abusive, not only toward other women but also toward men. Historically this has been somewhat rare. With the changes in the way women work and interact within our society, this appears to be on the increase. Instances of actual physical abuse of a husband are uncommon, but abusing and manipulating a husband verbally, sexually, and emotionally is well within the skill capability of most women. When women do become physical out of anger (not in self-defense), it is almost never with severe physical consequence. Typically, abusive women hit, slap, kick, slam doors, throw objects or push their husbands, but do not have the strength necessary to overpower a husband or inflict great physical harm as in cases involving abusive men.

It is true that an abusive wife may be more subversive or subtle than most seriously abusive men, but in the end her cruelty towards her husband can be as destructive as the more overt cruelty of an abusive husband.

Question: *I have been taught that it is my Christian duty to comply with any request my husband makes of me, no matter how cruel or demeaning or even terrorizing. Doesn't the Bible teach that wives are to obey their husbands "as unto the Lord?" If I disobey my husband, is that the same as disobeying God? I do not want to live in rebellion towards God, and I am willing to suffer if it be the Lord's will.*

Answer: Jesus said of Himself, "All authority hath been given unto me in heaven and on earth" (Matthew 28:18). God has absolute authority over all people, nations, and all of creation in Heaven and on earth. God's authority is not limited in any way. It extends to making life and death decisions, taking vengeance when and how He deems appropriate, judging the motives of the heart, or building up and tearing down as He decides. In contrast, all authority that God commissions to others is limited and subject to His own authority. No parent has the authority to command his children to murder a neighbor. No government has the authority to command believers not to preach the Gospel. No pastor has the authority to command his congregation drink Kool-Aid laced with Cyanide. No husband has the authority to command his wife to rob a bank.

Abusive husbands want to exercise their authority apart from submission to God's authority. In doing this, they break the chain of command that God has established for their family's protection as well as their own. This is a situation where, in military terms, they are guilty of dereliction of duty to obey a commanding officer or a law that has been put in place for the entire army to obey. Husbands are commissioned to exercise authority but they are also under a higher authority. While those who find themselves under the authority of a poor or very difficult officer must still obey him, it becomes the duty of a subservient soldier to respectfully appeal to, and disobey if necessary, an officer who explicitly commands him to violate the higher authority of the commander in chief.

In family terms, if a husband gives his wife an order that conflicts with that given by God, a wife is not to passively obey. By doing so she puts herself or other family members in jeopardy as a result. A wife is not released from the consequences of sinful decisions simply because it was the husband's wishes for her to condone sin or participate in it. Obedience to a husband's authority does not free one from a responsibility to obey God's authority any more than obedience to civil authority releases one from an obligation to obey God's commands.

As surely as God does not require us to submit to demonstrably evil commands, neither does He require us to submit to evil, sinful, God-dishonoring requests. Our bodies are the temple of the Holy Spirit, if indeed we are saved, and as such, they are not to be defiled (1 Corinthians 6:19–20). Therefore, we are to seek to preserve them in purity and holiness and have a duty to resist participating in anything that would defile us, even if such a request were a commandment that comes from a loved one who is in otherwise legitimate authority over us. If God calls us to suffer as a martyr for the faith and for righteousness' sake, unavoidably, then that is His holy will, but to submit to that which is demonstrably evil and that has nothing to do with the cause, name, or glory of Christ as a well-intentioned but misguided self-appointed martyr is anything but God honoring.

Question: *I can't figure out what triggers my husband's rages. It seems to always change. How can I avoid setting him off?*

Answer: As we have attempted to explain in some detail in this book, abusing a wife is sinful, never reasonable, and never justifiable. Sin is never reasonable, although it is sometimes quite predictable. But the irrational, unreasonableness of abusing one's wife by its very nature is only partially predictable at best. Since it is ordinarily impossible to predict what will set off an unreasonable person, trying to figure out, in detail, what sets a husband off is probably an exercise in futility. A better question, when one's husband becomes enraged, is to ask, "What duty does God's Word require of me in this difficult circumstance? Does God's Word permit me to return evil for evil?"

Question: *Why does my husband always want to move, just as we are getting used to a new school, church, etc.?*

Answer: There could be many different reasons for such behavior on the part of an abusive husband, but if a wife observes a pattern over and over of "pulling up stakes" and leaving as soon as there has been time to become acquainted with others, the reasons could be one or more of the following:

1. *He doesn't want his wife to develop any close friendships which might ultimately result in her intentionally or unintentionally revealing to someone else that she is abused.*

2. *He could be fearful of developing friendships in which that new friend or friends might suspect his sin problem.*

3. *He could be threatened by the thought of having to establish a stable and predictable lifestyle in which his controlling efforts would be harder to sustain.*

4. *He could be fearful that in a stable environment his wife could mature to where she would be less pliable or possibly consider the option of no longer submitting to his abuse.*

5. *He can obstruct flight if his wife decides to leave him, by preventing a stable environment that allows her to develop lasting and supportive friendships. In a stable environment in which there could be the development of lasting and supportive friendships if his wife decides to go, she might have a place to flee.*

Question: *My husband brags to our friends that we have a perfect marriage. Does he really believe this?*

Answer: The degree of self-deception necessary to live with oneself when he is willing to treat cruelly one he has promised to love and cherish, combined with the need to prop up an insecure and sagging ego with lies and distortions, combined with the almost universal trait of elaborate cover-up exhibited by abusive husbands, renders such behavior scarcely surprising when considered in light of these other traits. If an abused wife has been so terrorized that she is afraid to say anything for fear of retribution, an abusive husband may convince himself he has a good marriage—because she isn't objecting to anything. In any case, boasting about the (supposed) perfection of one's marriage disregards the spirit of the warnings in Proverbs 27:2 and 2 Corinthians 10:18.

Question: *I have been advised by the director of a domestic violence shelter to divorce my husband because she believes abusers never change. My friends all agree that this is what I should do. Should I file for divorce?*

Answer: Remember that you, not your friends, will live with the results of a divorce. Years down the road, your friends won't be there to answer your grown children's questions, or to comfort your heart. Therefore, seek Biblical principles that apply to your situation, not simply the opinions of others. Be fully persuaded in your own mind that you have wholeheartedly desired what God has desired and have done what is in the power of your hand to do to prevent divorce. The most precious thing at stake is not the marriage, but the soul of a husband who is in grave spiritual peril.

The standard advice given to abused wives by counselors with a non-Christian worldview is to immediately divorce and move on. They typically ignore what their own statistics reveal—that divorce doesn't always end the abuse and the abuser rarely goes away when there are children involved. While divorce is sometimes unavoidable, reconciliation and repentance of the abuser is always the better solution. Without Christ, it would be reasonable to say abusers never change. However, we serve a living God who can and does work in the hearts of the vilest men (and women). Only in the most severe cases would divorce be a righteous resolution and then only after careful consultation and oversight by one's pastor. Even in the rare circumstance where this would offer appropriate and necessary protection, we would encourage such a wife to remain single so long as there is any hope of repentance and reconciliation by God's miraculous power.

There are several reasons why we keep divorce off the table in all but the very worst abuse cases. First and foremost, the Word of God teaches us that God hates divorce. This fact is not a vague concept but a clear revelation described in the Bible. Yes, we know that divorce happens because not every human being cares about what God loves and hates and the majority are bent on rebelling against His good and gracious laws. No abused wife can *make* her husband honor God or do what is right! Nevertheless, because our God does delight in repentance and transformation by His grace and power, we want to wait rather than impatiently give up too soon. He is glorified when mercy and forgiveness are the desire of our hearts, just as it was in the heart of Christ for his abusers when he was so cruelly tormented on the cross of Calvary. Yes, admittedly it is a small number of abusive men who repent and thus experience the life changing transformation we long for, but we *have* witnessed many amazing examples of this in the lives of those who did believe and obey God's Word. After many years of counseling abuse cases we have learned that we can't predict who will or will not believe the Word of God and be changed by its power. Therefore, we want to give every abuser the opportunity to hear God's truth and experience the longsuffering nature of genuine love that is willing to wait and entreat patiently.

A second reason we do not encourage divorce is because there are many long-term consequences to this decision.

(1) Abused wives tend to have a sensitive conscience that is often tormented with guilt years after the divorce, particularly when they acknowledge they may have reacted too soon without sufficient patient waiting or made the decision to divorce merely to please family or friends.

(2) When grown, children often question their mother as to why she divorced their dad. It is extremely helpful when she can reply, "I did not seek a divorce. That was wholly your father's decision." All evidence of abuse as well as loving efforts to reconcile need to be saved so adult children have accurate information that will enable them to understand what happened.

(3) In cases where small children are involved and would not be protected by the court, it is sometimes wise for an abused wife to prayerfully weigh whether her children would be put in grave danger without her presence in the home during court ordered visitation with the father. Courts do not typically honor a child's preferences until they are in their teens and assumed to be old enough to speak for themselves. Unless an abused wife has clear evidence of criminal abuse toward the children, or evidence the

children would be in danger with the father, the courts will almost always grant 50/50 custody arrangements.

(4) When men refuse to submit to counseling and reject God's solutions to their sin, they typically file for divorce at some point. If a divorce is filed after a wife has carefully applied the principles of Matthew 18, we would say, as Paul did, "If the unbelieving depart, let him depart." (1 Corinthians 7:15) If a divorce is filed by the husband, a wife needs to secure a lawyer and seek an equitable settlement that takes her future as well as the future of her children into consideration. Under no conditions should a wife take a passive stance in the face of an unrighteous dissolution of the marriage. However, neither should she ever resort to ungodly, angry responses that bring shame to the name of Christ.

5

CLOSING THOUGHTS FOR VICTIMS

Perhaps your husband began acting out of character, a little peculiar, volatile or unpredictable shortly after you were married. You may have shrugged it off with an explanation, while inside your heart you harbored nagging fears. And now your worst fear has become a reality. You may now have indisputable, concrete evidence that your husband is not simply difficult or "stressed" but abusive and angry to the point of being dangerous. It isn't just a fear or nagging anxiety with no concrete evidence—it is an indisputable reality. Your head may be spinning with questions while your heart feels as though it is breaking in a thousand pieces. Perhaps you feel the ravages of anger one minute and gut-wrenching sorrow the next. One thing is certain—the pain you are experiencing is unlike anything you have probably ever felt in your life, and amidst all the turmoil whirling around in your head, you are very likely wondering, "What in the world am I going to do now?" Let's start with a few basic principles that are consistent no matter what your circumstances and then go over other suggestions which are variable, depending on your situation.

The purpose of this booklet has been to help you with the first steps in responding to an abusive spouse. It is written to the woman who is a committed Christian who wants Biblical direction, not simply generic information about domestic violence. Because we are believers who deeply desire our Lord's involvement and guidance, we turn our eyes toward Him as we move forward. Unlike the world, we know that "our help is in the name of the Lord, who made heaven and earth (Psalm 124:8). Therefore, we do not make decisions without praying and carefully weighing all in the light of the scriptures.

THINK AHEAD

Think your way through a few simple things. Remember what you do today and how you respond to this treacherous sin right now impacts your future life and the lives of your children and your husband. In fact, it can impact several people who will all be affected by choices you will make in the next few days or weeks. People (especially your children) will remember and look back on the way you handled this crisis. They might not understand or react now, but they will put the pieces together as they grow up, and they *will* remember things said and done. Your attitude will be remembered with clarity.

In times of deep anguish, raw emotions and fuzzy thinking commonly prompt people to say and do things they regret ten years down the road. Sadly, many women who have experienced just what you are experiencing today wish they would have done things differently. Some regret doing nothing at all until a deadly attack forever changed their world. Others wish they could take back words that were spoken and many unwise decisions that were made in anger. They can never take back their inactions, actions or words, but you do not have to become like them. You can do things differently because you are not ten years down the road—you are here, dealing with something that is happening right now, and you can handle this crisis in a way that not only demonstrates faith in Christ and honors Him, but gives you the best possible chance of a good resolution.

Remember that you have no control over what your husband is doing or how he chooses to respond when confronted. You might wish you could force him to make the right choices, but you cannot. What you can control is you. It is in the power of your hand to control what you do and say, and how you respond to his sin. Concentrate on doing what you know to be right, regardless whether your husband chooses to do what is right. Do it humbly, as unto the Lord, not self-righteously. No matter what he does or says, keep your focus on saying and doing what you know is the right thing. Resist the temptation to freeze in fear and not respond when you know you must. You are not responsible for his decisions to sin or his reactions to your decisions—but you are responsible for the way you react and the decisions you make in this very difficult time. This will be important for you to remember at *every step of the way*. Again, concentrate on you, not him. Focus on what is right and what God tells you to do in His Word. Commit your husband to the Lord and ask God to deal with him, and then make up your mind you are going to confront this and deal with it in a way that God can bless—regardless of your husband's threats or decisions. If you choose to handle it your way instead of God's way, you will be on your own. God never blesses sinful ways of responding to sin, even when the sin is as grievous and destructive as this one.

WHOM WILL YOU TRUST?

Before you do anything else, spend time alone with the Lord. He will be your partner and closest friend during this crisis, but you must follow His directions. Do not let your emotions dictate your actions. Decide right up front that God's Word will guide you, not your fluctuating emotions. As good as emotions are, they are not predictable or dependable and are never to be your determining factor when making decisions. Let God's Word be your navigation when the seas are stormy, and the fog is so thick you cannot see where you are headed. God's Word will never fail you if you will handle it carefully and seek wisdom on God's terms. Remember the Lord is your good Shepherd and will lead you in the way you need to go, but you must be willing to follow and listen to Him. He will not force you, but He will warn you plainly and entreat you with love and kindness to do what is right.

If you rely upon your own reasoning alone, the Word of God declares you are a fool. Proverbs 28:26 says, "He that trusteth in his own heart is a fool: but whoso walketh wisely, he shall be delivered." God promises to bless those who put their trust in Him, but those who trust in their own wisdom and lean on others, apart from God's Word, invite trouble and destruction. In Jeremiah 17:5-9, we read a contrasting story of two people.

One trusts the Lord, and the other trusts in human strength and reason. The one who trusts the Lord is happy, blessed, flourishing, and fruitful like a tree planted by a river. The one who trusts the human heart is cursed, empty, dry and directionless, like a tumbleweed blowing in the desert. Right now, each of us is as close as he or she chooses to be to the Lord Jesus Christ. We either trust Him and follow His Word, or we trust our own abilities to make decisions and follow our instincts. How about you? You are about to embark on a bumpy journey that will lead through some pretty stormy weather. Who and what will you follow when your heart says one thing, and the Lord clearly says another?

When King Asa turned to the Lord in a time of life-and-death crisis and relied upon Him, God delivered him from his enemies. Later, in his old age, he relied upon a country that hated God rather than trusting the Lord to deliver him from enemies that once again threatened him. In 2 Chronicles 16:8-9, we read the words of the prophet who was sent to confront Asa with his sin. He said, "Were not the Ethiopians and the Lubim a huge host, with very many chariots and horsemen? yet, because thou didst rely on the LORD, he delivered them into thine hand. For the eyes of the LORD run to and fro throughout the whole earth, to shew himself strong in the behalf of them whose heart is perfect [or right] toward him." Ask yourself now—who or what you will depend upon during this time of great trial? Will it be your heart? Will it be the words of friends and family? Or will you rely upon the Lord and trust Him? Talk this over with the Lord and make your choice before you go any further.

PREPARE YOURSELF

Remember that your husband is looking for excuses to justify his actions and he will seize any opportunity you give him to resent you and accuse you. The nature of guilt and an unrepentant heart is to shift blame on something or someone else so one does not experience the full impact of his sin against God. He may very likely blame you for his behavior and point out sins and failures you have or have not committed against him. While you may indeed be guilty of sinful behavior or carelessness within your marriage, absolutely nothing you have done causes his cruel anger or excuses his chosen sinful solution to his or your problems. An angry man is angry no matter who he is married to. One is not excused or justified for abusing others for *any* reason. It is very important for you to understand this because your husband may openly accuse you to others to win sympathy, and sadly, some people will fall for the trap. Again, do not worry about him or others; be concerned only with yourself and how you respond. Memorize Romans 12: 21, "Be not overcome of evil, but overcome evil with good."

SATAN'S TRAPS

One of the most difficult problems you as the offended wife may experience is the temptation to react as though your husband's anger is a personal rejection of you. He is not rejecting you—he is rejecting the Lord and the Lord's way of dealing with life's problems. This thing did not happen overnight—it began when he was very young and learned sinful ways of getting what he wanted and handling problems. The habits of anger fester and grow into something quite exaggerated in the mind of an angry person. Like other men who believe the lies of the evil one, he may be convinced he is on the path to happiness, when in fact he is on the path to disillusionment and sorrow. Remember, Satan does not make the trap obvious—he always hides it in something that looks good. Where Satan will trip you up, if you are not wise, is getting you to focus on your deep hurt, rather than the best way to respond. When you are suffering unjust treatment at the hands of one you deeply love and trust, it is very easy to slip into morbid self-pity and debilitating anger or depression. Do not do it! Turn to the Lord and find comfort in His arms. He will sustain you and enable you to handle this wisely if you stay dependent upon Him! Cast all your care upon Him, for truly, He does love and care about you (1 Peter 5:7).

Another trap Satan attempts to use is that of minimizing one's own sin by comparing it with someone else's sin. While you are not to assume guilt for your husband's sin in *any* way, you do need to examine your heart and humbly admit any sin you know you have committed against your husband. The principle of Matthew 7:1-3 is always to examine your own heart first and deal with your sins before you confront another about his sin against you. You will want to ask your husband's forgiveness for your sin, but you must not accept blame for his sin or ask forgiveness for behavior not sinful by God's definition. You are responsible for your sin, regardless how or why others sinned against you.

DON'T BECOME ANGRY WITH ANGER

Remember you will be prone to using anger to vent your outrage and grief. Do not react to your husband with anger! You may be grieved and brokenhearted, but do not let anger or hatred poison what you are about to do! As much as you possibly can, separate your emotions from the sin and proceed with quiet reliance upon the Lord. Your anger will never be used by God for good and will never be blessed, so resist the urge to yell and accuse in anger! "For the wrath of man worketh not the righteousness of God" (James 1:20). Never forget that God does deal with sin and *will* discipline your husband. You do not need to do this. The Bible says, "Dearly beloved, avenge not yourselves, but rather give place unto wrath: for it is written, Vengeance is mine; I will repay, saith the Lord" (Romans 12:19). Do as Christ did when he was horribly mistreated and refused to return evil for evil. Commit yourself and your case to God, just as Christ did, for our Heavenly Father judges righteously (see 2 Peter 1:18-23).

This is that point where you will need to follow God's directions rather than the human emotions gripping your heart. The human response when you are hurt is to retaliate and hurt back. This might feel good for a moment, but it does not help your marriage or your personal walk with the Lord, and is not blessed by God. Direct the emotional energy fueling expressions of anger toward resolving the problems you face—do not direct it toward your husband. When anger seems to be overwhelming, get alone with the Lord and pray until your spirit is under control. The emotion of anger is human, but its expression can be sinful and destructive. Let God respond with vengeance if He so chooses—He can do it without any kind of sin; we cannot. Remember the Lord can deal with your husband much better than you can.

Review and memorize this acrostic from Chapter 4:

C *ry to the Lord.*

L *ean on Christ for mercy, grace, help.*

A *ct Biblically. (Overcome evil with good. Use God-given resources.)*

S *peak softly, but truthfully.*

H *arbor no grudge—don't retaliate.*

Ready, set, go

If you have come this far and believe the Lord is giving you grace to move to the next step, begin thinking about enlisting the help and support you will need. If you do not need to flee immediately to escape imminent danger, take time to plan carefully.

PREPARATIONS

- *Enlist support and counsel.*

- *Decide where you will live during a separation.*

- *Gather documents – Children's passports, etc.*

- *If you have evidence such as phone records, letters, bank records, or receipts, make a copy of them and seal them in an envelope. Put the originals in another envelope and place them in a safe place where your husband cannot find them. You may need to give this envelope to someone to keep for you temporarily.*

- *Keep a journal (online in cloud). This is VERY important! It is admissible in court as evidence, provides a timeline later.*

IMMEDIATELY BEFORE SEPARATING

- *Secure money in a separate account.*

- *Remove your name from any credit cards.*

- *Make sure bills are paid.*

CONFRONTING WITH A PLAN

- *Enlist competent help.*

- *Do not confront your husband with your children present, even if they are in another room. If possible, enlist family or a friend to watch your children overnight.*

- *Sometimes abusive men will switch from one type of response to another when the first doesn't succeed in getting you to do or react as he wants.*

- *Typical reactions: Shock, embarrassment, denial, "hurt" (or) anger, counter accusations, intimidation, threats, or demands for divorce (or)remorse, crying, self-flagellation, threats of suicide, "apologies."*

LIST OF SUGGESTIONS

- *If you received eye-witness evidence from another person, make sure they know you are confronting your husband and telling him exactly from where the report came. Ask if they are willing to validate the information if need be.*

- *Do not be distracted with cruel or pessimistic statements. Ignore them. Do not attempt to defend yourself in any way. Refuse to argue. It is a dead-end path and does not help.*

- *He may agree to counseling, or he may refuse to consider it. Explain that you need counseling and are seeking it whether he chooses to join you or not. Let him know your desire is that he goes with you, but it must be his choice.*

SEPARATION

- *My advice is to stay put whenever it is possible to do so. If you stay in your home, ask a family member to stay with you. Change your locks immediately.*

- *If your husband has threatened harm in any way, seek shelter in a domestic violence facility or a place where you cannot be found.*

- *Once you have confronted a dangerous husband and have left your home, do not reenter for any reason. Ask for a police escort to go back into your home to retrieve needed articles.*

THE AFTERMATH

- *It is possible your husband will immediately repent and desire reconciliation with you. While this is a wonderful response, it does not mean the problem is resolved. Many sins underlying abuse need to be addressed. Your husband's desire to immediately put the sin aside and forget it happened increases the probability of repeating the sin. For his sake as well as your own, seek out help as soon as possible and go, whether he goes with you or not. If he is serious about changing his course, he needs to talk to someone who is able to deal with his sinful anger and abuse. Insist on this, even if you grant forgiveness and desire to resume a normal life.*

WHAT IF HE FILES FOR DIVORCE?

If your husband files for a divorce, he has basically begun a legal lawsuit against you. You must retain a lawyer to protect yourself to the degree you can do so. Do not assume this move means there is no hope. It is certainly a formidable obstacle, but not one that is impossible. You need to handle this crisis gracefully, just as you wish to handle a confrontation gracefully. Retain a lawyer, contend for what is just, and do not acquiesce or fail to protect your assets or properly prepare for your future. At the same time, do not permit your lawyer to become vindictive or ask for more than what is a just division of property and assets. To the degree you can do so, keep the relationship peaceable. Sometimes lawyers make the contention worse and drive a bigger wedge between you and your husband. Do everything you can to keep this from happening.

Never give your husband cash; always write a check, and always keep receipts and records of every financial transaction you make with your husband or anyone. Never assume your husband is going to "take care of you" financially simply because he vowed he would. A man may say this initially as a way of relieving guilt, or say it to comfort a wife. In fact, it is very, very common. It is NOT common for an abusive man to actually do this. Most do not. Once a husband is emotionally severed from his wife, he can turn against her as well as his children with incredible callousness and cruelty. You might want to believe the best and put your trust in comforting words, but do not do it. Keep Proverbs 26:24-25 in mind. "He that hateth dissembleth with his lips, and layeth up deceit within him; When he speaketh fair, believe him not: for there are seven abominations in his heart."

LOOK FORWARD, NOT BACKWARD

You may wish a thousand times or more you could go back to a happier time or could wake up and find this is just a bad dream. Accepting what happened takes time, and the wounds inflicted will be very painful for a long while. We wish we could give you a formula that would erase all the horror and heal the deep wounds inflicted on your heart in an instant, but we cannot. Only One can heal your wounded heart and bind up those wounds. Speaking about the Lord Jesus Christ, the psalmist said, "He healeth the broken in heart, and bindeth up their wounds" (Psalm 147:3). I cannot heal your wounds, but I can urge you to go to the One who can, and I can testify that all who do so find Him faithful and true. Your Savior will never betray you, say an unkind thing to you, or abandon you. He is tender toward a person treacherously betrayed by a spouse, and He will take you up and care for you when those who should have protected you failed. Stay close to Him, make your Bible your bed buddy, and talk to Him continually. He is the one friend who can get you through this and restore the sunshine in your life once again. Trust Him! Remember that *no one* can predict what will happen next—just keep your eyes on what you need to do *right now*, not two days from now, next week, or next month. God will direct you one step at time, one day at a time, and will give you the grace and strength you need moment by moment as you deliberately put your trust in Him and rely on Him to help you.

APPENDICES

APPENDIX A
Seeking Capable
Biblical Counseling

As we have previously explained, many well-meaning pastors and other church leaders do not have a demonstrable competence in the understanding of, or dealing with, spousal abuse. Consequently, finding a capable local counselor may be difficult. The following suggestions for doing so are carefully offered.

First, and above all, make your search a matter of fervent prayer, remembering God's guidance in Proverbs 3:5-7.

Second. Call at least three local, well established local churches, which claim conservative biblical commitment in theology and practice, and ask them for one or more recommendations for finding a certified, biblical counselor nearby.

If one or more are recommended, call them and ask them to state the key principles underlying their counseling, and how they apply them.

If they insist on marriage counseling first, go no further. On the other hand, if they insist the abuse must be dealt with first, and when the abuse has been dealt with, then problems in the marriage, ask for an appointment.

If this fails to provide a counselor, we recommend that you go online and search for organizations which claim to provide biblical counsel for abuse.

When you find such a listing, we suggest asking the questions included above.

APPENDIX B
INFORMATION ABOUT SHELTERS FOR BATTERED WOMEN

Local police departments are more than happy to provide numbers of shelters for battered women in a prescribed area. The woman must make the phone call to the shelter, not the counselor, as she will be interviewed by phone before they will agree to take her. When the woman calls, she will be gently questioned by another woman, and if there is available space in the shelter, she will be given a time and place to meet a taxi which will take her to the shelter. The address of the shelter is never given so as to insure safety for the women being protected there. The meeting place is usually the local police station. Normally, women are not allowed to bring their cars to a shelter. It is wise for a wife in this situation to drive her car to a safe residence where she can leave it and can be assured of having access to it if she needs to make a change or leave the shelter.

If a woman is forced to flee her home suddenly and has not been able to pack a suitcase for herself and her children, she will need to ask the local police department for assistance in escorting her to her house to retrieve needed clothing, medication, and so on. If this is done, one officer will usually ask the husband to wait in a separate room while another officer allows the wife to pack her things. The officers will stay until the woman has left. If the woman has children, it is wise to make sure they do not accompany her on this visit home. Have them stay with someone who is capable of providing care and support at such a stressful time as this.

It is wise for an abused wife to make sure she has withdrawn enough money from her bank account to cover her expenses. The woman is not charged for staying at the shelter, but money may be needed immediately when she leaves. It is very common for abusive men to withdraw all money from accounts or close all accounts once they become aware their wife is separating or seeking help. The wife should not withdraw more than half of anything in a joint account with her husband.

Most shelters allow women and dependent children to stay up to thirty days. She may leave at any time she chooses, but she is not encouraged to do so unless it is considered safe. When she is ready to leave, she will be taken back to the arranged drop-off point. Women in shelters are not normally allowed to use a phone unless they are supervised and then only for five to ten minutes. They will not allow the woman to disclose her location to anyone, including her church or counselor.

While at the shelter, food, clothing, and necessary needed attention will be provided. The shelter will also provide licensed counselors who will attempt to educate the woman regarding domestic violence and other issues such as "self-esteem." Usually videos depicting typical cases of abuse are shown and discussed. The women are encouraged to talk about the nature of the abuse they have suffered and are encouraged to file restraining orders which volunteers help her submit if she chooses. They usually encourage, but do not force, her to do this. Some shelters also provide information about legal separation or divorce procedures, and some provide access to lawyers who volunteer their services. Biblical counselors who encourage the use of a shelter ought to prepare a woman, as much as time will allow, for the type of counsel she will receive and the most gracious way to maintain her Christian focus and commitment.

Most shelters anticipate the needs of women and children and provide toys, games, and activities to keep them occupied. It is wise for a woman going to a shelter to take along Christian material for both her and her children to read. She should take her Bible and helpful Bible studies for both her and the children. Christian videos and tapes are also helpful as these will not usually be available to her. Women and children living in a shelter will not normally be allowed to attend church services.

It is extremely important that the woman's husband be notified that his wife and children are in a shelter just as soon as she is safe. The best method is for a pastor and at least one other deacon to accompany him on a visit to the house in order to talk to the husband about the situation. It is sometimes helpful for the wife to leave a *brief* note for her husband, explaining her actions and her desire for counseling intervention. The woman needs to remain in the shelter until either alternative arrangements can be made for her that insure her safety, or until a period of time has lapsed and the husband is agreeable to leaving the home for a period of separation while initial counseling is taking place, or until it is considered safe for the woman to live with her husband.

APPENDIX C
REPORTING VIOLENT ABUSE

We can think of no circumstances, or Biblical truths, which would prevent a pastor, deacon, elder, or other concerned helper from promptly reporting an incident of violent abuse to the police. Indeed, in most of the states it is now a criminal offense to fail to do so, and church members who intervene or church officers who assist in a "cover-up" in order to keep a husband out of jail can themselves be charged with a more serious criminal offense.

For many, if not most abusers, police intervention is the only means of bringing an abusive man to the place where he will acknowledge the seriousness of, and reality of, his criminal behavior. This follows the Biblical admonition in Romans 13 and again in 1 Peter 2, establishing judicial authority as a God-given means of dealing with criminal behavior.

> *Let every soul be subject unto the higher powers. For there is no power but of God: the powers that be are ordained of God. Whosoever therefore resisteth the power, resisteth the ordinance of God: and they that resist shall receive to themselves damnation. For rulers are not a terror to good works, but to the evil. Wilt thou then not be afraid of the power? do that which is good, and thou shalt have praise of the*

same: For he is the minister of God to thee for good. But if thou do that which is evil, be afraid; for he beareth not the sword in vain: for he is the minister of God, a revenger to execute wrath upon him that doeth evil (Romans 13:1–4).

Submit yourselves to every ordinance of man for the Lord's sake: whether it be to the king, as supreme; Or unto governors, as unto them that are sent by him for the punishment of evildoers, and for the praise of them that do well (1 Peter 2:13–14).

Reporting criminal abuse is a wise option for an abused wife for many reasons. First, it often provides a sufficient enough jolt as to wake an abuser from his delusion that what he is doing "isn't that bad." Second, it gives the wife additional protection in the event he should contemplate revenge for reporting him in the first place or a repeat of the crime. Third, it establishes a record of the abuse, which proves to be invaluable in the event she should ever separate from her husband on a long-term basis or be forced by her husband to go through a divorce hearing. Without established proof of abuse (e.g. hospital records, police report), she would not be able to prevent her husband from being granted joint custody of the children, or of having unsupervised visitation with the children. And fourth, allowing the judicial system to exercise its authority in the case insures the abuser will be forced to submit to counseling for an extended period of time. On numerous occasions, the authors have successfully petitioned the courts, as Biblical or pastoral counselors, for all the court-ordered counseling. It is not unusual for a judge to order the abuser to submit to all counseling sessions required by the Biblical counselors, normally for one year, with the instruction that the church is to notify the court immediately if the abuser fails to keep the appointments except for a doctor's excuse for illness. Any failure to keep the counseling appointments results in the issuing of an immediate warrant for his arrest and results in jail time. This can be a valuable, legitimate (godly) "leverage" to motivate a husband to participate meaningfully in the counseling.

We do add a caution to those who decide to help a wife who has been assaulted by her husband and has called for police assistance. When the police arrive, or when she is taken to the police station, not surprisingly, she may deny the abuse, even if exhibiting bruises, cuts, and other signs of physical violence, attributing them to a fall, to bumping into the edge of a cupboard door, and so on. Such denial most often arises out of terror as to what her husband will do to her when he is released from (the usually brief) custody. She may also panic or "feel sorry for" her husband as she realizes the severe consequences an arrest or conviction will have on her husband and on the family. Counselors need to note, also, that the husband will usually be furious about police intervention, and will blame his wife for the hardships this choice is going to bring upon him (and upon the family) until he fully comes to himself and experiences complete repentance. It will be a challenge for the counselor or pastor to bring both the husband and the abused wife to understand that it is not the wife who has brought such hardship and humiliation on the husband, but the husband's choice to commit a crime against his wife. He must come to accept complete responsibility for the action, or he will likely torment the wife with her decision to enlist the help of the police.

Still another caution to counselors: To expect the police to consistently be able to protect an abused wife if she returns to dwell with her husband, once he has physically abused her, is an exercise in sentimental insanity. A wife in such circumstances needs (along with children who cannot defend themselves) to be taken into a safe place *immediately*, and arrangements made, if she is willing, to have a restraining order implemented as soon as possible.

A final note—if she is willing, have photographs taken of all signs of physical abuse, *immediately*. In all probability, these will prove to be an invaluable tool in helping a repentant abuser to face the seriousness of his sin, as well as providing critical evidence if the whole matter, as we have indicated above, ends up in the civil court system.

APPENDIX D
CHURCH INVOLVEMENT WITH
A SERIOUS ABUSE CASE

In Romans 15:14 Paul remarks "And I myself also am persuaded of you, my brethren, that ye also are full of goodness, filled with all knowledge, also able to admonish one another."

The verb *to admonish*, in the Greek is *noutheteo* which means to lovingly confront (about one or more observed sins) for the purpose of effecting change in behavior. In Ephesians 4:11–16, Paul more fully expressed the remarkable concept that the God-intended norm in healthy, vibrant congregations which are growing in the Lord spiritually and numerically, should be an accepted responsibility on the part of communicant *members* to confront, to admonish, to encourage, to warn, to instruct one another for the purpose of growing in grace. And all that activity is not carried out just by the pastor, but by well-trained, godly members, whether they are officers in the church or not. Including other church members in the counseling process greatly reduces the occurrence of problems that stem from the abuser's ability to keep the offense a secret. Once it is more open, the abuser has a much greater motivation to deal seriously and honestly with the problem, receive the healing benefits of having the love and support of others, as well as the benefits of increased accountability which is so helpful to long-term victory.

Sadly, this high calling is not only rare in believing churches in our age, but rejected outright by many sincere Christians, even pastors. Christians for the most part have not been trained to assist one another in seeking resolution to end problems Biblically. Consequently, an abused wife who is a believer, and who ought to be able to entrust herself to those who are tasked by Scripture to protect her (the leaders in her church) may find that they neither believe her testimony, nor understand the severe difficulties she faces in extricating herself from a very serious situation that can be unhealthy to her and sometimes life-threatening.

As noted elsewhere in this book, it is not uncommon for well-meaning pastors who sincerely want to be faithful to Scripture (e.g., 1 Corinthians 7:1–16) to give a God-fearing wife no option but to go back to her husband with some version of the instruction "try harder" or "be more submissive" beginning with (of course) working on correcting her own sins (Matthew 7: 3–5). However, this approach, while ordinarily the proper approach in virtually all other counseling situations, can be detrimental or even fatal to the abused wife, when there is ample evidence of irrational rage, unpredictability of abuse, and other high-profile behavior which strongly indicates an abusive relationship. At that point, *protecting the endangered,* those who cannot help themselves, must take precedence. This, of course, is the more difficult approach and removes from the pastor or other Biblical counselor, the relative ease of a single-text, single-issue solution. In many

Bible-believing circles, this approach may expose such an individual providing that kind of careful awareness of Biblical priorities (e.g., we are to save life in such a situation, not contribute to destroying it) to attack from other believers for such counsel.

What then, is an abused wife to do? There is no easy answer, but praying for the Lord to provide another individual who can see the problem, and understand it in some measure, is a great start. If the wife doubts her pastor's grasp of the subject, she could ask such an understanding friend to simply ask, in general terms, what the pastor understands about dealing with this kind of a problem and if he appears hesitant or unsure of himself, he could then be asked to help locate a competent Biblical counselor elsewhere. But in any abuse counseling situation a Biblical pastor, or elder, deacon or trained Biblical counselor should not become involved unilaterally, but always seek the assistance of another responsible member of the congregation, not only for the protection of the one ministering to the abused wife, but also to meet the requirements of 2 Corinthians 13:1.

In a congregation where at least some members and officers have received a measure of ongoing training in dealing with matters involving wife abuse, that wife is blessed indeed, and may, in fact, find superb support. Our desire is that every Bible-believing congregation would be so equipped, since this abuse problem tragically is widespread, and the involvement of the church family as a corporate body is invaluable in helping both the victim and the offender come to see the love and power of God working on their behalf.

APPENDIX E:
THE SERIOUS ISSUE OF
DIVORCE

We have acknowledged the fact that an unrepentant abusive husband may choose to divorce his wife when she refuses to once again submit to his abusive treatment of her and/or the children, even if she does not desire to be divorced. Most Bible-believing churches acknowledge that in such cases, a godly sister is "not under bondage" (1 Corinthians 7:15). However, what exactly that means can be in serious dispute among godly brethren, and we have elected to leave the interpretation of the meaning of that phrase to those churches which reverently and carefully seek to be faithful to God and His Word within the context of their doctrinal standards. After all, if a rescued wife chooses to live under the protection of the church which was instrumental in her deliverance from real peril, then she has an obligation to abide by the interpretation and application of that congregation's theological position on 1 Corinthians 7:15.

But what of the wife whose abusive husband increases his threats to do her bodily harm, who regularly disregards legal restraining orders intended to protect her, who continually harasses her in numerous ways the police cannot deal with apart from a court order, who threatens to kidnap the children, and so forth? What needs to be established by those in spiritual authority over a godly wife in the situation described here is whether or not she is in real danger of being maimed or even murdered.

This is not an easy question to answer, just as it is difficult to figure out when a suspected terrorist will decide to commit a suicide attack. Yet, the godly advice to see evil before its visitation, and to hide oneself (Proverbs 27:12) is pointless, if not cruel if, in fact, God has not given us both the license and the ability to project the likelihood that an evil man (or men) will commit a given evil. That is especially true in those cases when specific threats have been voiced. So if a corporate decision is made (2 Corinthians 13:1) to increase the protection of an abused wife who has received threats of murder or bodily harm, and divorce will significantly increase that protection, then the requirement to preserve life over-rules the Biblical prohibition of divorce, just as the commandments to obey God over-rule the commandments to obey the civil authorities (e.g. Romans 13:1-7; I Peter 2:13-15) when those people make a law or ruling which contradicts one or more of God's commandments.

And, in the end, if the clearly abusive husband eventually repents, and in the opinion of at least two or three competent witnesses that repentance is substantiated by long-term fruit ("suitable for repentance"), that couple of course can re-marry.